Into Abba's Arms

© Thomas R. Golden 1992.

Into Abba's Arms

Finding the acceptance you've always wanted

SANDRA D. WILSON PH.D.

Tyndale House Publishers, Inc.
WHEATON, ILLINOIS

The American Association of Christian Counselors is an organization of professional, pastoral, and lay counselors committed to the promotion of excellence and unity in Christian counseling. The AACC provides conferences, software, video and audio resources, two professional journals, a resource review, as well as other publications and resources. Membership is open to anyone who writes for information: AACC, P.O. Box 739, Forest, VA 24551.

Visit Tyndale's exciting Web site at www.tyndale.com

Cover art by Melinda Schumacher

Designed by Melinda Schumacher
Edited by Lynn Vanderzalm

Library of Congress Cataloging-in-Publication Data

Wilson, Sandra D., date
   Into Abba's arms : finding the acceptance you've always wanted / Sandra D. Wilson.
     p. cm.
   Includes bibliographical references (p.   ).
   ISBN 0-8423-2473-9 (sc : alk. paper)
   1. Spiritual life—Christianity. 2. God—Love. 3. Intimacy (Psychology)—Religious aspects—Christianity. 4. God—Fatherhood.
I. Title.
BV4501.2.W5634   1998
248.8'6—dc21   98-3012

*With love and gratitude beyond telling,
I dedicate this book to the glory of my Abba God—
the only true father I have ever known.*

CONTENTS

A new wind is blowing. For now it's only a gentle breeze, a whisper quietly stirring a growing company of people to think they could actually *experience* God.

Experience God—not merely know truths about him, but with unmistakable clarity sense his presence, hear his voice, rest in his love—even in the middle of unbearable struggles and deep emotional wounds.

By God's mercy, I am among that company of Christians whose hunger has been sharpened by suffering, that company of long-term Christians who have somehow been graced with just enough humility to admit we don't know God as deeply as he longs to be known—and can be known *before* we get to heaven. I'm among the growing number of people who have no choice but to realize that the path we've walked for a long time isn't leading to the depths of intimacy we yearn to share with God.

Like Dr. Sandra Wilson, I've been trained to sit across from hurting people, to listen with a mixture of genuine compassion, professional distance, and theory-guided insight, and to do, then, whatever a therapist does to "treat" emotional disorders.

Also, like Sandy, I'm a Christian who thinks that the gospel— that incredible opportunity Christ provides to walk into the

Father's presence and to find that he's deliriously glad, thrilled, delighted we're there—speaks as nothing else does to the core issue beneath our emotional struggles.

And I hope that, like my much valued and deeply respected friend Sandy, I'm finding a new path into the safety of Abba's arms, a path that saints through the ages have already walked, a path described long ago in Scripture.

Into Abba's Arms is really Sandy's story, the story of a woman brave enough to let herself feel a hunger for more than what her understanding of walking with God provided; a woman brave enough to confront the depths of her emotional pain and intractable sin in the presence of a God she didn't know all that well; a woman brave enough and balanced enough to appreciate all that she had learned before about helping people and knowing God as she began to open her hungry heart to experiencing God more personally than ever before; a woman humble enough to passionately enjoy a relationship between a never-abandoning Father and a needy, scared, and insecure child.

The result of Sandy's journey, reported with winsome candor, is a growing healing from emotional wounds—a healing that is a by-product of her much greater joy in experiencing God more richly.

Imbedded in these pages is a fresh paradigm for Christian counselors, a paradigm that *must* be taken seriously: Don't merely *tell* yourself the truth; *experience* the truth, firsthand, in your soul. Both her autobiographical record of how she's doing it and her advice on how we, too, can do it ring true to what I know of the Spirit's ways. But more, this book is an invitation to every Christian to dance in the presence of God, to stand before him with no masks, naked and needy, confident of his delight.

God has used Sandy to help me dare to believe that he is wildly excited to call me his child and to whet my appetite for even more of what he offers. The path she illumines is the one I have recently begun to walk, too often with trembling and inconsistent steps. But thanks to her, I walk it with renewed confidence that the Father is waiting with outstretched arms for me to come home.

Read this book with your heart open. God's Spirit may use it to lead you home.

Dr. Larry Crabb

ACKNOWLEDGMENTS

What a remarkable journey this book has been! And what a joy to have been able to make it with the wonderfully supportive people at Tyndale House. Many thanks to Ron Beers, Ken Petersen, and Meg Diehl for the role each has had in helping me along the path.

But I especially want to thank Lynn Vanderzalm for her light and loving editing and her gentle but persistent encouragement to follow where Jesus was leading. Lynn never doubted that God was doing something important in me and in this book, despite the unforeseen changes he was making in both me and my writing.

I started out to write a book primarily about abandonment issues but also about the Lord. However, *he* wanted this to be a book primarily about cultivating intimacy with Christ but also about abandonment issues. And it took me a while to discover that! I'm so thankful that Lynn and others cheered me on in that discovery process.

I am also very grateful to Dr. Larry Crabb for his encouraging and eloquent foreword.

As always, I owe an enormous debt of gratitude to my husband, Garth. Throughout my writing, I have been sustained by his love, his patience, and his faith in me and in what God was calling me to do.

Having said all of the above, my highest praise and gratitude belong to my heavenly Father. To paraphrase Zechariah 4:6: It is not by encouraging support or skillful editing but by my Spirit, says the Lord of hosts. And God's Spirit has faithfully guided, strengthened, comforted, and beckoned me on in my journey toward Abba's arms.

1 "Why Do I Have a Hole in My Soul?"

Have you ever known people who seem to have holes in their souls? Nothing seems to satisfy these people for long—no sensation, achievement, or relationship. That's how it was for Claire.

For as far back as Claire could remember, her cold, angry mother told her that she was ugly and that no man would ever love her. Those repeated comments poked holes in Claire's soul. So the love and approval Claire *did* receive from friends and even from her father kept leaking away in a sense of rejection. The truth of her unique worth and keen intellect trickled out of Claire's awareness, leaving her parched for attention and affection.

Soon after finishing college, Claire met Karl, a handsome, intelligent older man. When he expressed romantic interest in her, Claire was astonished and head over heels grateful. Though she had known Karl for only a few months, she eagerly accepted his proposal of marriage.

Immediately after their simple wedding, they moved across the country from New England to Arizona. Claire was thrilled when she got pregnant a year or so later. But her joy turned to dismay when Karl insisted she have an abortion, especially since that was decades before abortion was legalized. Claire convinced Karl that she would never go to an abortionist. Before long, he had staged several gun-cleaning "accidents" that nearly killed Claire and their unborn child. Claire was terrified and confused, not knowing any reason for her husband to behave as he did. As it turned out, Claire didn't know a lot of things about Karl.

Claire didn't know that before he met her, Karl had abandoned a wife and several children and had embezzled money in a scheme that involved the postal service. Those charade-shattering facts came to light when federal authorities caught up with Karl at the very time he was trying to kill Claire. Stunned by the devastating new information about Karl, she watched in shock as he was arrested, convicted, and imprisoned.

Claire never saw Karl again. She destroyed all his photographs and letters. So the child he abandoned before birth never met her father, never heard his voice, never saw his picture or even a scrap of his handwriting.

I am that child. A child born into a legacy of abandonment and shame. Just like so many of you.

Talk about abandonment and rejection! There was my mother, in 1938, three thousand miles from her family, not legally married, with a fatherless newborn daughter. She already had a very wounded self-concept because she had felt rejected by *her* mother. And at the hospital where she worked, rumors raced that she had never been married. I wept when she told me shortly before her death in 1990 that she had tacked her marriage license to the hospital bulletin board to quell those rumors.

Mother had to work to support us, so she found an elderly couple who would rent us a bedroom, provide meals, and care for me during the day. These well-meaning but emotionally barren people gave me custodial care but no secure sense of belonging. In reality, I *didn't* belong.

When I was about two, my mother met and married—again hastily—the man she hoped would be a real father to me. I was ten before she told me he was my stepfather. Once again, my mother didn't know something very significant about the man she had married: he was an alcoholic.

For my mother, this second disastrous marriage heaped shame on shame. She began to look to me to be a very special, remarkable child, for that would validate her worth as a good person and parent despite her choice of husbands. I started piano lessons when I was four years old, and I was playing in public at the age of five. That early launch into a performance lifestyle shaped my life profoundly.

I worked very hard to be the best at everything I did because that seemed to make my mother happy. And happiness is in short supply in alcoholic homes. Besides, when my mother was happy, she seemed more emotionally available, which made me feel more secure. So I learned how to take care of her so it would feel as if she were taking care of me.

In the next few years, my stepfather's alcoholic episodes of violence escalated. Much of my memory of my childhood is blank, but I remember crawling out a window onto the porch and spending the night with neighbors because my drunken stepfather had bashed down the door to get into the house.

Other traumatic memories returned after being buried out of my awareness for decades. I remember being sexually molested by my step-uncle. There were several other isolated molestation episodes. One involved a trusted family friend. Another was a classic sort of "stranger-danger" situation that most children these days are taught to avoid.

When I was thirteen, my mother and stepfather divorced. While my stepfather stayed marginally involved in my brother, Ron's, life, I never saw my stepfather again after the divorce. So I was abandoned by the only father I had ever known.

You've probably guessed that fear of abandonment and father-loss issues have been major sources of pain in my life. You're also probably not surprised to learn that my approval addiction has been focused primarily on winning approval from men in positions of authority (otherwise known as *father* figures).

Sometimes my husband, Garth, gets caught in the crossfire of my battles with abandonment. A few years ago I experienced a classic "emotional flashback" triggered by not seeing Garth where I expected to meet him in a shopping mall. An emotional snowball started rolling, getting larger and more overwhelming by the minute as I jogged the length of the mall searching for him. By the time I found him, I was sobbing like a child. Naturally he was thoroughly baffled by the whole thing. So was I.

Later, as I thought about what had happened, I remembered all the times as a kid when I had waited for my mother to pick me up from one place or another. Sometimes she was very late, and I panicked, wondering how I would take care of my little brother and myself. That seems almost laughable to an adult. But to an overresponsible, insecure child, it's deadly serious. After all, she was the only caretaker who hadn't abandoned me. And although I had to perform to earn my place of belonging, at least that was better than not having a place at all.

When I was thirteen, I gave my life to Jesus, and he began giving me new life by revealing his Father's heart of love for me. God gave me a deep hunger for his Word from the moment I became his child. I've clung to verses like Psalm 27:10 that promise that even if parents forsake us, the Lord will "hold [us] close." Along the way, God has also used my wonderful family, loving friends, and committed Christian counselors as his instruments of healing.

Scars of shame and abandonment still mark my life today. But not as deeply as they did yesterday. Self-focus, perfectionism, and people pleasing still cling to my soul like barnacles. But they are loosening their grip a bit.

In the past two years I have discovered in my relationship to God a depth and closeness I've never known before. In the next chapters I'll tell you more about how this happened. I'll also describe how increased intimacy with Christ is healing core abandonment wounds—those holes in *my* soul—at a depth I never dreamed possible.

HOLES OF ALL SIZES

Some of you may be struggling to relate to my story. Perhaps you were born into well-functioning, loving families. So your souls feel pretty whole, so to speak. Others of you might be thinking that my life has been a picnic compared to the trauma and abandonment from which you suffer. The holes in your souls feel roughly the size of the Grand Canyon—on your *good* days!

What has punctured the holes in our souls? Disobedience in the Garden, primarily. Disobedience and its resulting spiritual and relational alienation. For in the truest sense, the fall into sin was a fall out of relationship. It was a fall out of our secure place of belonging with God and into self-absorbed isolation and inner emptiness. It was also a fall into the abandonment we know from interacting with others who live in the same isolation and emptiness.

The abandonment we experience in relationships stabs more holes in our souls. Sometimes it happens in one life-shattering experience of betrayal by someone we love and trust. More often it comes from an accumulation of disappointing relationships. For example, you may have been unfairly dismissed, excluded, or passed over at work. Or

*In the truest sense,
the fall into sin was a fall
out of relationship.*

perhaps you were left behind, ignored, or just plain "dumped" in a friendship. You may have had a crushing experience of feeling rejected or abandoned by people in your church, people you assumed would be there for you.

Maybe your spouse has abandoned you, either by leaving you through separation or divorce or by ignoring you through emotional distance. As a result, you feel disillusioned, lonely, rejected, and abandoned.

And as if all this weren't enough, I believe our souls harbor a deep, nameless knowing that we were created for something far better, something unshakably solid and enduring. That "knowing" is what C. S. Lewis called our "lifelong nostalgia" to be reunited with our Creator.

With ancient echoes of Eden whispering in our souls, we've been longing for belonging ever since. And with our sinful self-wills screaming for obedience, we've been trying to satisfy that longing every which way but God's.

> *Ever since the loss of relationship in Eden, we've been longing for belonging.*

How does this longing for belonging play out in our lives? Bruce can tell you more.[1]

BRUCE'S STORY

"It's so strange. After more than twenty years in various ministries, I am only on the front edge of learning about life and about God."

That's how Bruce, a bright, dedicated, fortysomething Christian recently described himself. Raised with an alcoholic father and an extremely controlling mother, Bruce grew up trying to earn a place of belonging by saving his family. Not just saving the family's reputation by being successful enough to bring honor to it. Bruce worked to save his parents' marriage, to end his dad's drinking, and to earn his mother's respect for his individuality. Unsuccessfully. And it seemed that no matter how hard Bruce worked, it was never enough to quiet his gnawing sense of insecurity and loneliness.

However, his childhood served as invaluable on-the-job training for the parachurch ministry Bruce joined right out of college. Its goal was to save the *world*. And Bruce rose in its ranks to become the leader in the top section of the organization.

"I was always driven to be one of the best—no actually, *the* best. And as I look back on it, I realize my compulsion had virtually nothing to do with any passion for the gospel. I was driven to earn acceptance and respect. I believed that being a Christian put me on the winning side. But I really didn't believe God thought much of me. And to tell the truth, I didn't spend much time thinking about God. I was afraid of what I might discover. Besides, I stayed too busy earning a name for myself."

Eventually another prominent ministry hired Bruce to organize and lead its national conferences. However, within a few years the ministry collapsed. At the same time, Bruce's emotional and relational struggles created the pain necessary to push him toward healing changes in his life.

Several years away from that now, Bruce says, "I've been forced to slow down, get a little saner, and learn to love my wife and kids, who—-amazing as it might seem—really love me. And I'm beginning to trust with my heart that God is who I've believed he is in my head."

In the chapters ahead, we'll hear more about Bruce's journey toward the belonging he's always craved. We'll also learn that we don't have to grow up in troubled families to struggle with the fear of abandonment that fuels our deep relational longings. That's because relationships—consistent, genuinely caring interactions with other human beings—are not just icing on the cake of life. They are its very substance.

ABANDONMENT AND OUR LONGING FOR BELONGING

We need to take fear of abandonment seriously because God takes it seriously. Consider that in nearly all of his "fear not" statements, he adds, "for I am with you." God speaks to our fear of abandonment by telling us to call Jesus "Immanuel"—God with us. I believe that's because he knows that our fear of abandonment is rooted in the reality of who we are.

> *God speaks to our fear of abandonment by telling us to call Jesus "Immanuel"—God with us.*

When we are young children, abandonment equals death—literally. So in a sense, we are *physically* predisposed to fear of abandonment at the nucleus of every cell. But we are relational beings, too. So fear of *relational* abandonment, which may *feel* like death, stalks us long after we can keep ourselves physically safe. And, of course, all of us this side of Eden face spiritual abandonment because sin separates us from our Creator. That deadly separation creates the possibility of *ultimate* abandonment, which, come to think of it, may fairly well describe hell.

This all means that even if we grow up in healthy families with loving parents, we're still vulnerable to feelings of abandonment and the anxiety they generate. And this vulnerability can stir up in us feelings of shame because it makes us feel "grown-down," like stupid, helpless little kids. When that happens, we're likely to think there's something uniquely wrong or weak in us. After all, we live in a society that prizes independence and self-reliance.

Facing the depth of our relational longings makes us feel fragile, fearful. That's why we usually don't face it. Instead, we distract ourselves, often with professional accomplishments and material possessions. We pursue success and "stuff." That's what Eric did.

Eric, a prominent physician in his late forties, has an enviable reputation—and a profound sense of loneliness. Reflecting on his current life, Eric said, "People respect me and my work. They say I'm a success. But I still feel cut off from others. I know I should be happy. I know people envy me. So why do I feel so much like an outsider wherever I am? I have spent so much time and energy on professional achievement that I don't have any left for really connecting with people. My marriage died from neglect. My children seem like strangers. And my colleagues feel like enemies. Do I feel lonely? At times I feel so lonely I could die."

Others of us distract ourselves from our longing for belonging by focusing excessive attention on relationships.

Those relationships eventually become unhealthy and unsatisfying because we use them to substitute for relationships with ourselves and with God. That seemed to work for Gloria for years.

In her midfifties, Gloria looks every bit the comfortably kept wife she has been for over thirty years. When her husband suddenly moved out (and *in* with a young associate), Gloria's upscale world collapsed. This is how she describes it: "My husband, our children, the house. That was what I lived for. I can't tell you how hard I worked to get everything just the way he wanted it—the meals, the parties, the vacations. All I wanted to do was please him. And he tossed me aside like cold oatmeal when he found a *hotter* dish. I try to stay angry, which is what my friends tell me to be. But mostly I feel like a lost, scared little kid. What am I going to do now? The children are grown and have lives of their own. I feel so utterly alone."

Carla also depends on relationships to make her feel safe and worthwhile. Twenty-eight and single, Carla lacks the confidence and the social skills to build solid relationships. She lives in chronic loneliness, near the edge of despair. "No one knows how lonely I feel at work. Sometimes I just want to scream, 'Does anybody know I'm here?' But I feel even lonelier on the weekends when I actually see more people around me and know that not one of them really cares about me. It's worst of all on Sunday. Maybe I'm too naive or something, but I hoped and prayed it would be different at church. I mean, there I am with people I see week after week, and no one seems to notice me. Aren't people supposed to care about each other at church? I guess I just expected it to be like a family. I *need* a family!"

these situations seem familiar? Probably so,
_an beings harbor a God-designed yearning
_u need to belong. We all need intimate relationships.
That explains the mountains of evidence demonstrating
that throughout our lives we need consistent, caring interactions with others to develop our senses of identity, to
learn how to relate to others responsibly, and even to be
physically healthy.[2]

The God-designed importance of close relationships
may also explain why we feel dismayed—even hurt and
frightened—when important people in our lives ignore,
dismiss, forget, reject, abuse, or abandon us. To be sure,
their actions my cause economic and other hardships. But
if we could listen to the heartbeat of our distress in the
wake of those experiences, we would hear the sighs and
cries of relational longing.

And that's the last thing some of us ever expected to
encounter.

BLINDSIDED BY ABANDONMENT

Many of you grew up in basically healthy homes in which
your parents did a good job of providing safety, stability,
and acceptance. So you knew you had a place where you
belonged.

Not that healthy families never have problems. *All* families have problems. If your parents were wise, they knew
this, so they faced their problems and got help to solve
them. Of course, even in healthy families, you probably
experienced some situations that left you feeling abandoned because even the most loving caregivers cannot
meet all our needs all the time.

Sometimes people raised with a solid sense of belonging are blindsided by abandonment in their adult lives. That's what happened to Sam when his wife left him.

A high school English teacher in his late thirties, Sam still sounds shell-shocked when he talks about his divorce two years ago. Since his mom and dad were happily married, Sam was sure he would be, too. Now Sam isn't sure about anything. He tells it like this: "Maybe it sounds too melodramatic, but I feel betrayed. My wife and I promised before God to be together 'till death do us part.' I know *I* meant it. I assumed my wife did, too. I shared more of myself with her than I did with anyone else in my life. And it wasn't good enough. *I* wasn't good enough! Well, I can tell you this: never again. I won't risk being that vulnerable with anyone ever again. But the thought of never loving anyone or being loved again makes me feel indescribably sad and lonely."

After his divorce, Sam found some measure of comfort and encouragement during visits with his parents. But what if it's our parents who suddenly decide to abandon us?

Carolyn grew up with a silver spoon in her mouth and a deep love in her heart. From the first moment she heard about Jesus at church, Carolyn loved him. Passionately. Her wealthy, well-educated parents attended church regularly but never got "carried away" (to use their term) as Carolyn did. They assumed their bright, beautiful daughter would go from a top Ivy League school into a prestigious professional position.

But Jesus and Carolyn had other plans. This is how she explains what happened as a result: "When I was in high school, I got active in a Christian organization that helped focus my love for Christ. I knew I wanted to go into full-time ministry of some kind. Of course, that nearly killed my parents when I told them. The thought of their daughter 'begging for money' to raise support for a salary was too much for them. They said I had to choose between them and 'this obsession with religion.' I thought they were just trying to scare me, but they were serious. So I chose. And now I'm not welcomed in my family's home 'until I come to my senses.'"

Carolyn is working her way through a state university and is sharing an apartment with three other Christian young women. She also works with a parachurch ministry whose staff has become a kind of substitute family. Still, Carolyn weeps as she fumbles for words to describe the pain she feels because her parents have rejected her.

Carolyn was an adult when her parents abandoned her. How much more painful it is for people whose parents abandoned them when they were children.

ECHOES FROM CHILDHOOD

The more severe and frequent our childhood abandonment experiences, the greater our lifelong sensitivity to any situation that triggers similar feelings. As a result, many of us organize our lives around this crippling fear of abandonment. And we usually have no clue we're doing it.

Our childhood abandonment might have been the *hands-off* kind, like chronic neglect. Or maybe it was verbal and emotional mistreatment. Accumulated experiences like those contribute to our abandonment anxieties. After all, it's pretty tough to feel a secure sense of belonging when the adults we depend on for nurture and affection aren't supplying either very consistently.

Ellen remembers pleading with her parents to play with her or read to her, but they were always too busy with "kingdom work." They never seemed to have time simply to sit down and listen to Ellen when she wanted to talk about what confused, delighted, or frightened her. And when she complained about their disinterest, she was given a sermonette about her selfishness in the face of all the needy people in the world without Christ.

> *The more severe and frequent our childhood abandonment experiences, the greater our lifelong sensitivity to any situation that triggers similar feelings.*

Years later, when her husband began to exhibit the same kind of workaholism, Ellen panicked inwardly. Instead of speaking the truth in love to her husband and working toward greater marital intimacy, she responded as she had in childhood. Ellen begged for attention until she eventually gave up and threw herself into her own busyness.

Ellen's hands-off abandonment took the form of benign neglect. Other children experience it more from a steady barrage of verbal put-downs like "You'll never amount to anything" or "If you weren't so lazy, you could get the kind of grades your cousin gets." And word bombs like these blast holes in the souls of youngsters who receive them.

Sadly, some children also receive profound *hands-on* abandonment through physical or sexual abuse. Such betrayals by trusted authority figures traumatize children and create expectations of abandonment. Hands-on abandonment leaves children feeling ineligible for anything else. Just ask Kristin about that.

Thirty-one-year-old Kristin often wears long-sleeved clothing and dark glasses—even on summer nights. "It's so strange, you know. My husband swept me off my feet when I met him. He said he couldn't live without me and pushed for us to elope when I'd known him only a month. He was so jealous of any other guy's attention to me that I just knew he'd treat me like a queen. What a joke! It didn't take long after the wedding to find out who ruled in our house. And it sure wasn't me. I wanted to leave the first year when he started beating me and screaming filthy accusations at me. But my parents and my church would have been horrified. Then I got pregnant and felt I had to stay. I've spent thirteen years feeling trapped, scared, betrayed, ashamed, and lonely. I feel utterly hopeless."

Kristin's physical abuse from a rage-aholic father trained her to tolerate disrespectful and dangerous behavior. So her future husband's possessiveness and jealousy didn't set off alarms in her mind as they would have if she had seen an affectionate relationship between her parents or if she had received loving nurture from them. Instead, her boyfriend's behavior all seemed so familiar and "right."

Whether we first experienced abandonment or neglect as children or as adults, those realities mark each of our lives. And many of us have been earnestly seeking relief from that crushing burden in biblically based books, tons of tapes, and countless conferences.

While all these resources can be helpful, I believe that

we experience healing from wounding relationships only as we experience healing intimacy with God. I pray that this book will help you in your journey toward that healing.

> *We experience healing from wounding relationships only as we experience healing intimacy with God.*

BACK TO BELONGING

In his book *The Longing for Home*, pastor and author Frederick Buechner notes that the word *longing* comes from the same root as the two words *long* (meaning length) and *belong*. He says, "In its full richness *to long* suggests to yearn for a long time for something that is a long way off and something that we feel we belong to and that belongs to us."[3]

And as Buechner observes, this longing for home is so human, so universal, we give it a special name: *homesickness*.

> All of us are homesick for Eden.
> We yearn to return to a land we've never known.
> Deep is the need to go back to the Garden,
> A burning so strong, for a place we belong,
> A place that we know is home.[4]

Those lines capture the theme this book will resound: We long to go home where we belong! Even when we've never known a home where we felt as if we belonged. *Especially* when we've never known a home where we felt as if we belonged! We long to be fully at home with our heavenly Father, who created us and to whom we can most securely belong. We yearn to plug the holes in our souls.

There's gloriously good news for all of us hole-in-the-soul Christians who yearn for greater closeness to God. *God* wants us close to him even more than *we* want to be close to him! How do I know? Because he plants a part of himself, the Holy Spirit, in each of his beloved children. God's Spirit acts, in part, like a homing device, sometimes beeping softly, other times shrieking deafeningly in our hearts to direct us back to where we belong—in God's eternal embrace.

> *God's Spirit acts, in part, like a homing device, sometimes beeping softly, other times shrieking deafeningly in our hearts to direct us back to where we belong—in God's eternal embrace.*

I believe that the gospel's "goodest" news proclaims this: The way back to that original heart-to-heart relationship with God has been opened—*by God himself.* In isolation from himself. Abandoned by himself. On a cross.

And, as we will see in the following pages, God patiently continues to beckon us back to belonging.

Moving Closer

As you think about what you have just read, take some time to reflect on your own situation. You may want to record your thoughts in a notebook or journal. Use the questions at the end of each chapter to help you move closer to God.

1. Did you identify with any of the people in this chapter? If so, with which person? Why?

2. In what ways have you felt abandoned or betrayed or neglected?

3. In what ways do you feel like an outsider who doesn't belong?

4. What do you most long for in your life? How are you trying to fill that hole at the moment?

5. Take time to write *your* story, as I wrote mine for this chapter. Do you see themes of rejection, of abandonment, or of not belonging? If you do, please don't despair. I promise you that there is hope for healing the wounds that come from the experiences you've identified.

6. Ask Jesus to begin to make his presence real in your heart in a deeper way than ever before.

Moving On

In this chapter we've seen that God created us with a need for relationships and that this need expresses itself in our longing for belonging. We've also seen how painful relational experiences in childhood or adult life can deeply wound us.

In chapter 2 we find the only source of deep healing for those deep wounds.

2 "Why Do I Try So Hard but Change So Little?"

As Christians we're usually proud of our solid theology. But our shaky hearts and relationships are another story. We feel guilty for not living in the "peace that passes all understanding" that we know—complete with chapter and verse—God promised his children (see Philippians 4:7). We're disappointed in ourselves for not having a consistent sense of our Savior's abiding presence.

What's more, when we are aware of the pain from the holes in our souls and the scars of abandonment, we feel alone, like outsiders who long to belong—to God and to other people. And some of us feel so empty inside. Or at best we feel uncomfortably insecure in situations that include even minor rebuffs.

It's not supposed to be like this! After all, we're Christians.

We want things to be different, but we're not sure what to do. Some of us have been pursuing personal change for quite a while. Yet many of us also know that we have not *substantially* changed—deep down in the innermost core of our beings. So we're frustrated. And tired.

What's wrong with this picture? Or perhaps the better question is this: What's wrong with our ideas about change?

FAMILIAR FORMULA FOR CHANGE

When most of us think of changing, we think of correcting our misbeliefs, our thinking patterns. That makes sense if we believe that the rational part of us is the core of who we are.

Many people helpers have taken this approach. Typically they also address spiritual needs and encourage people to turn to God as the power source for their changing processes. Over the years that's been my approach to facilitating change.

The Truth about Abandonment

I feel upset and scared right now because something happened that reminded me of how alone and terrified I sometimes felt as a child. I don't like this feeling, but I know that I will survive experiencing it and it will pass.

The truth is that *as an adult,* I cannot be abandoned in the same way I could have been as a child because I now have resources that I did not have then.

The truth is that I may get passed over, stood up, forgotten about, left behind, ignored, "dumped," and even cruelly rejected, but I will survive all of these painful experiences.

The truth is that as God's beloved child, I have his promise that he will never leave me, forsake me, or abandon me. I can rest safely in his faithful love.

For example, in *Released from Shame*, I encouraged readers to write a statement of truth like those in the preceding chart to help correct misbeliefs that create painful feelings of abandonment.[1]

"Thought correctors" like this can be enormously helpful to us. Our belief systems do significantly shape our emotions, our choices, and our behaviors. In fact, Jesus said in Mark 7:20 that all attitudes and actions flow out of our thought-lives: "It is the thought-life that defiles you. For from within, out of a person's heart, come evil thoughts." Clearly, replacing lies by learning truth will always be a critical part of change.

But how do we learn truth deeply enough to change deeply?

I've been wondering recently if we have been going at change from the wrong direction. I have come to believe that before we can know truth at a transforming level of deep change, we must experience it in the context of *relationship*. In essence, that's what God demonstrated through the change model he used.

> *Before we can know truth at a transforming level of deep change, we must experience it in the context of relationship.*

GOD'S MODEL FOR TRANSFORMING CHANGE

God delivered transforming truth in a *relational* package— the person of his Son. That truth came in the form of One with whom we can have an intimate relationship.

We experience deep change through the *Person* who is Truth, not by merely believing *precepts* of truth. Truthful propositions remain vitally important for us to learn, memorize, and assimilate into our belief systems. And this happens most effectively in intimate relationship and dialogue with a person—ideally with the One who names himself Truth.

> *We experience deep change through the Person who is Truth, not by merely believing precepts of truth.*

Think about this question: Where did we learn the lies that pollute our belief systems? We learned them in the presence of those who mattered to us—in dialogue with people. We heard the lies spoken, we saw the lies lived, and we experienced the effects of the lies within relationships. For example, we may have been told repeatedly that "men are only out for sex" or "women are only out for money." If we have absorbed these lies, then our expecations of relationships have been affected. Or perhaps we saw our parents live the lie that financial success matters more than anything else in life. And now we may find ourselves living that same lie and teaching it to our children in the process.

We learn the truth in the same way. Someone has said that we do not change when we stay alone.[2] That's why one-on-one mentoring, discipleship, and counseling will always be more powerful than the best organized, most eloquently presented seminar (or book!) in the world.[3]

Of course, ultimately we want to be able to speak the truth to ourselves. Yet those of us with past abandonment wounds are apt to become too overwhelmed with fear to remind ourselves of truthful precepts convincingly enough to make a difference deep within. We're so easily confused and discouraged when we're trying to change. Because we need modeling, affirmation, and lots of encouragement to stay with the hard work change requires, I believe that the presence of a trustworthy, caring person is the key to deep, life-transforming change. This means that we need to apply our Creator's relational model of *spiritual* transformation to *every* area of our lives where we seek genuine change.

> *Why can't we get the biblical truths we know in our heads down to our hearts?*

What's more, the relational wrapping of transforming truth may help to answer a question that has troubled many of us for years: Why can't we get the biblical truths we know in our heads down to our hearts?

FROM THE HEAD TO THE HEART

Some truths don't need to make that arduous head-to-heart journey. I use basic mathematical truths to balance my checkbook without experiencing a deep personal connection to them. But then I can't say I've been transformed on any significant level by mathematical truths either (as my bank can confirm!). Even some *biblical* truths—for example, the names of Jacob's sons—don't need to grip our hearts, so to speak.

The relationship with truth required in balancing checkbooks and memorizing biblical names differs dramatically from learning to relate to God as a loving Father, developing a sense of secure belonging, or restructuring our relationships with important people in our lives. Discovering that has changed my life.

Over the past two years I've experienced a healing of my deep feelings of abandonment, and the healing has been more significant than I ever thought possible this side of heaven. In effect, the pathway from my head to my heart opened. Wide. And I am now experiencing an unshakably secure sense of belonging that years of Bible study, consistent prayer, and intermittent counseling failed to produce, even though each helped me to grow.

What happened? My friend Gary Moon gave me a copy of his first book, *Homesick for Eden.*[4] As I read it, I ached to experience God the way Gary said he had learned to experience him. I sobbed in regret for never knowing there were spiritual habits, usually called "disciplines," to help me realize that possibility.[5] I sobbed for joy at the possibility that I could learn them. And I began to practice some of the spiritual habits that Christians through the ages have used to deepen their awareness of God's real presence in their lives. (Especially the habits, or disciplines, of silence and solitude.) Immediately my routine "quiet times" exploded and disappeared.

Reflecting on it now, I think most of my previous devotional times were spiritual sunscreen applied as quickly as possible each morning to protect me from overexposure to the day's sin. Or to use another image, my quiet times were sort of "Jiffy Lube" for the soul, a practice intended to keep everything running smoothly. My devotional times routinely included two elements: (1) Scripture reading structured to accomplish a certain amount by a certain date, and (2) prayer, which meant me talking and God listening.

You'll notice that this kind of devotional time doesn't leave a lot of room for relationship building. It is rather like reading a close friend's letters when the friend sits beside you, then talking without letting that friend speak. True, I knew a lot about God's Word, which taught me quite a lot about God. But for the most part, that knowledge stayed wedged in my intellect. There wasn't much "trickle-down effect" to my heart to secure me when abandonment assaulted my shaky sense of belonging.

Like many sincere evangelicals, I had settled for learning denominationally determined definitions of theological terms *about* God instead of learning how to have an increasingly intimate relationship *with* God.[6]

But all that is changing.

> *I had settled for learning denominationally determined definitions of theological terms* about *God instead of learning how to have an increasingly intimate relationship* with *God.*

PRACTICING GOD'S PRESENCE

As I read about believers who found heart-to-heart intimacy with Jesus Christ, I kept seeing the phrase "practicing the presence of God."[7] The phrase was strangely mystical to my Baptistically tuned ears, to be sure. Yet I knew it was thoroughly biblical.

From the outset of my Christian life, I had been taught that, by his Spirit, Jesus was in me and with me even as he sits at the right hand of his Father in heaven. And I believed it. I just didn't know how crucial it was to transfer that head belief into heart experience. Consequently, I hadn't actually focused on the unseen but *real* presence of Christ right there with me in my devotional times. Or anywhere else. And I had little sense of intimacy with the Savior.

Genuine relational intimacy doesn't develop quickly. Or accidentally.

We need to cultivate an environment in which intimacy can flourish. And we do this by practicing habits like listening to and giving undivided attention to the person with whom we want to be close. As we practice such habits over time, we really get to know someone. Relational intimacy grows.

That process applies to a relationship with Jesus, too.

How close and intimate would a human friendship be with someone who never spoke directly to us? Not very. In our relationship with God, the problem isn't that he doesn't speak; it's that we are often unwilling to listen.

In his book about prayer, Eddie Ensley quotes from fourteenth-century believer Catherine of Siena on this point. When asked why God no longer conversed with his children in the personal way he did in the past, Catherine replied: "God is no longer as personal as He once was because instead of treating Him as the Master and seeing ourselves as the disciples, we treat Him as the disciple and act like we are the Masters."[8]

Ensley goes on to say, "In short, instead of praying, 'Speak Lord, your servant is listening,' we pray, 'Listen Lord, your servant is speaking.'"[9]

I've already admitted that most of my prayer life reflected this attitude. Of course, I never thought of it in those terms. And I would have been shocked and offended if someone else had suggested it to me.

> *In our relationship with God, the problem isn't that he doesn't speak; it's that we are often unwilling to listen.*

Spending time with God in solitude, experiencing the reality of his presence, and cultivating inner quietness create the condition in which we can hear him more clearly. And as we share our hearts with God and hear him share his heart with us, our relationship grows deeper, closer. More *real*.

That's how friendships work.

LISTENING TO GOD

If you had asked me a few years ago if I ever heard God speak to me, I would have given a nebulous response. I have never heard a Charlton Heston–type bass voice booming out of the clouds. Nevertheless, over the years, I have occasionally discerned the Spirit's inaudible voice speaking in my thoughts. Better, higher, and wiser than my own thoughts, these gentle impressions on my heart encouraged or admonished me in ways that drew me nearer to heaven.

And as we share our hearts with God and hear him share his heart with us, our relationship grows deeper, closer.

But I knew nothing of how to make "listening prayer" an intentional part of my time with God. I was deaf to "the very voice of the Father . . . the living voice of God that enters the heart," as Andrew Murray describes it in his classic *With Christ in the School of Prayer.*[10]

So I began purposefully placing myself before the Savior to let him do some of the speaking in our prayer conversation. After all, a conversation is supposed to have *two* sides. I decided to record parts of these "holy conversations" in my spiritual journal (which is just a fancy name for a notebook with a mission).

For example, one morning I was meditating on the truth that God the Son allowed himself to be temporarily but truly overcome (he *really* died). He did that so he could overcome the sin and death that would—without him— eternally overcome us. As I murmured my stunned appreciation, I "heard" these words:

> **You are just beginning to get an inkling of what I mean when I say I love you.**

> *I mean, I really love you!*
> *You matter to me.*
> *Those times when you are most enthralled—*
>   *most moved with love for me—*
>   *are but a dim reflection of*
>   *how much I love you.*
> *I love you enough to let you walk away from me*
>   *so that when you return—and you will,*
>   *as you know—*
>   *you will experience even more of my love.*
> *And no matter how wonderful,*
>   *how loving and merciful, you come to know I am,*
>   *I am far more.*

Another morning God spoke this to the "ears" of my heart:

> *Child,*
> *You are learning to rest in me as well as to listen*
>   *to me.*
>   *This is good.*
> *Keep practicing. You will need it.*

As I wrote that last sentence, I felt a pang of fear. *Need it?* For what? Almost immediately, God responded to my unvoiced anxiety as these words formed in my thoughts:

> *Don't be afraid—*
>   *I will always be with you, Child,*
>   *really present with you as I am*
>   *really in you by my Spirit.*
> *I am the strong Daddy you need,*

> *the wise Daddy you need,*
> *the comforting Daddy, too.*
> *Trust me and my steadfast, loyal love for you, Child.*
> *I know you and what you need;*
> > *look to me, not to others, to meet your needs.*
> *Keep practicing the truth you know.*
> *All will be well.*
> *You are safe in me.*

Tender, personalized words like that draw my heart to God and deepen my sense of his real presence. They also make Scripture come alive.

LISTENING TO GOD IN SCRIPTURE

As I read the Bible now, I listen for God instead of checking off a schedule milestone. To prepare my mind and heart for hearing God in Scripture, I personalize passages with first-person pronouns. After reading and personalizing Ephesians 1:1-9 one morning, God spoke this to my heart:

> *"Grace to you and peace" are my gifts to you and*
> > *all my children.*
> *You have been seeking grace (a favored status)*
> > *from people,*
> > > *believing it will bring peace.*
> > > *It never does.*
> *Only entering more and more deeply into the*
> > *reality of my grace*
> > > *will bring the genuine peace of heart you are*
> > > > *dying for.*
> *I already died for it.*

> *And I rose so you would know it's true.*
> > *And I have the power to make it true for you.*
> *Hear me.*
> *Believe me.*
> *Learn to rest in the peace of my grace.*

Another day I incorporated Bible *study* into my devotional time. I usually separate study times from my early-morning times, which center on building an intimate relationship with God. Studying Scripture with commentaries and theological dictionaries spread around me tends to keep precious biblical truths locked at the intellectual level.

That morning I wrote this:

> *I'm transfixed by Ephesians 3:16-19.*
> *Went to Bible study tools to get better grasp on the words*
> > *know in verse 19 and love in Paul's writings.*
> *All that was interesting and inspiring,*
> *but the knowing of Christ's love that surpasses knowledge*
> *grows and is nurtured most for me right here,*
> *as I spend time with Jesus, talking and listening to him.*

Then I "heard" the following:

> *As you let me love you and tell you of my love,*
> > *you will be strengthened in your inner person.*
> *You can't be spiritually strong without deeply*
> > *knowing that*
> > > *I love you.*
> > > *You.*
> > > *Not just the world, but you.*

God's inaudible voice always speaks in agreement with Scripture. That's one way we know we're hearing from our Savior, not our adversary, Satan. (Of course, if we have extremely distorted images of God, we may find it very difficult at first to recognize his true voice.) Appendix A contains other guidelines to help us identify the source of what we hear with our inner ears.

As I continue to listen purposefully to God and to experience more of his love for me, my love for him grows in response. And he binds my heart and will to him ever more tightly. That's how Jesus said it works: Loving hearts become obedient hearts (see John 14:15, 21).

As I "descend with my mind into my heart" in times of solitude, God's presence and his promises make that journey, too.[11] As God's *presence* becomes real to me, God's *promises* become real. In much of contemporary Christendom, we have emphasized the latter without the former. I know I have. But for most people with significant abandonment issues, it hasn't worked.

As God's presence becomes real to me, God's promises become real.

I doubt that separating *relational* knowledge of the Promiser from *rational* knowledge of his promises ever truly "works." There's a kind of first-things-first principle operating here, I think.

FIRST AND SECOND THINGS

"You can't get second things by putting them first; you can get second things only by putting first things first," C. S. Lewis said.[12] Like many of you, I have tried living by the reality of the *promises* without living in the reality of the *Promiser*. Yet God designed a model of transforming change that inseparably couples the two. And we need to begin with him.

> *Like many of you, I have tried living by the reality of the promises without living in the reality of the Promiser.*

I believe that this first-things-first way of conceptualizing life-transforming change explains something that challenges and mystifies many of us. Why can some Christians who have, for example, lost a child eventually declare God's goodness and describe how they know—as never before—the reality of God's love and comfort? Does a child's death automatically produce that change? Obviously not. We certainly don't see it in everyone.

Such an unfathomable transformation comes when people bring their deep pain, anger, and grief right into the presence of God. As they practice the real presence of God by being real, by honestly pouring out their anguish and doubts, and as they listen to God pour out his heart to them, intimacy builds. And as the *Person* who is Truth becomes real to them, his *promises*, which are true, become real to them. Thus, God's *Word* comes alive as never

39

before because, in effect, *God* has come alive as never before.

Aren't you glad that we don't need to wait for catastrophes to drive us to our knees, hungering to hear from God? Whatever our present circumstances, we can begin practicing spiritual habits that will help us build an intimate relationship with our Savior. And in the context of that relationship, we will change deeply.

> *And as the Person who is Truth*
> *becomes real to them, his promises, which*
> *are true, become real to them.*

Perhaps you are like me and have been taught to focus on *learning* truths to correct misbeliefs rather than on *experiencing* truth in intimate friendship with Jesus, the Truth (see John 14:6). If so, transforming truth remains a theological certainty rather than a personal reality. The two are light-years apart—as far as head and heart.

When I began practicing spiritual "habits of the heart" to experience Christ's real presence, not only did my relationship with him take a quantum leap, but somewhere deep inside, the ancient ache of abandonment also began to subside. It was as if—for the first time—I met my Immanuel. Jesus, God with *me*, became real. So did his promises of eternally nonabandoning love.

I never anticipated what a profound change that would make in my life. Healing is the gift I am receiving, not the goal I was seeking. This, too, follows the first-things-first pattern.

This intimacy-with-Christ model of transforming change is not some sort of celestial *Let's Make a Deal.* You know: we spend an hour or so with God most mornings so he'll kiss away all our hurts. In fact, I believe *our* longing for unconditional love originated in the heart of *God.* His longing—if that is the right word, and I suspect it's not—is met perfectly within the Trinity.

As we spend time getting to know God—*really, experientially* know him—we will adore him for who he *is* rather than only thank him for what he *does.* Knowing, loving, and enjoying God must be our only goal. After all, that's why we were created.

Healing is the gift I am receiving, not the goal I was seeking.

RESULTS AND REASSURANCE

As Jesus has become increasingly real to me, he has become the rock-solid *center* of my life. I sense abundance and stability at my core, where I used to feel insufficiency and insecurity that often left me reeling from fear of abandonment.

I've always dreaded being alone. Now I *never* feel alone. I've always avoided silence. Now silence nourishes me. I no longer click on the television the moment I enter my hotel room when I'm traveling. (I'll describe other changes in coming chapters.)

Perhaps this concept of experiencing transforming truth *relationally* sounds too touchy-feely, too anti-intellectual. After all, didn't the apostle Paul say in Romans 12:2 that we are to be transformed by the renewing of our minds? Indeed, he did. And before Paul wrote that, God had him spend a lot of time and parchment focusing squarely on Christians' secure place of belonging in God's family. This is especially evident in chapter 8 of Romans. Clearly, if we are serious disciples, we present our sin-darkened minds to God for renewing. But we are to present our *total* selves to Christ, not only our intellects (see Romans 12:1).

Maybe this practicing the presence of God business seems too mystical—if not downright heretical. Part of the problem may center on vocabulary. For example, many Christians recoil from the idea of *meditation* since for many of us that word comes laden with a lot of New Age baggage. Visions of Shirley MacLaine contacting her "spirit guide" or some other deadly spiritual practice spring to mind. I share your concern. We must avoid Eastern meditation that focuses on withdrawing from reality and emptying our minds. However, I believe that the dangerous counterfeits need not keep us from the very real blessings gained by filling our minds and hearts with God's presence and Word.

Listen to J. I. Packer describe the meditation I practice and advocate:

> Meditation is a lost art today, and Christian people suffer grievously from their ignorance of the practice.

Meditation is the activity of calling to mind, and thinking over, and dwelling on, and applying to oneself, the various things that one knows about the works and ways and purposes and promises of God. *It is an activity of holy thought, consciously performed in the presence of God, under the eye of God, by the help of God, as a means of communion with God.*[13]

Practicing—or concentrating on—the reality of Christ's presence with us can also be called private worship. In his book *How to Worship Jesus Christ*, Joseph Carroll writes of how learning to worship Jesus by entering "into the very presence of God" revolutionized his devotional life.

Instead of looking at my watch and saying, "I have ten minutes to get through my prayer list," I simply knelt down and quietly meditated on the fact that I was in the presence of the Lamb of God and worshiped Him. My quiet times then became something for Him, not something for me; and with the . . . pouring of my heart to Him in worship, came the overpowering awareness of His presence.[14]

Carroll is describing truth's journey from his head to his heart. He moved from theological certainty about Christ's presence with *all* believers to experiential reality of Christ's presence with *him*.

To some evangelicals, practicing the presence of God, and other spiritual disciplines, sounds too much like "works" added on to our grace-based salvation to earn more of God's love. We must get this straight: God doesn't demand that we practice these spiritual habits to be his children. They neither *earn* us more of his grace and love nor *secure* our place in his family. They do, however, create the condition that allows us to *experience* more of his grace and love and our secure place in his family.

HELEN KELLER AND ME

Living with feelings of abandonment or rejection or neglect is a bit like dealing with a handicap. The sense of abandonment impairs our ability to grow into and live out of the truth of God's love. If that is true, then I am an impaired person. Maybe you are, too.

Practicing God's presence has built a handicap ramp to my soul. It allows God's transforming truth to come rolling down from my head into my otherwise inaccessible heart. And this heals and changes me at a level nothing else ever has. Strange as it sounds, I also relate more personally to one of my all-time heroines because of this.

> *Practicing God's presence has built a handicap ramp to my soul.*

Helen Keller's remarkable life captivates me. Biographers tell us that Helen became blind and deaf after she was severely ill at the age of two. They also describe how Helen's mother told her daily that her parents loved her. The mother lamented that Helen could not understand because "[her] eyes are closed, and [her] ears are stopped." To respond to

Helen's need, her wealthy father hired a creative instructor, Annie Sullivan, who came to live with Helen and teach her how to communicate with the world beyond her perpetually silent night. With patience and tenacity, Annie pressed Helen to practice and master sign language and braille. As she did, Helen made contact with the world around her and began to experience her parents' love.

I think we're a lot like Helen Keller: spiritually blind and deaf to some degree even after we're born into God's family. At great cost—the life of his Son—God the Father provides us with a Teacher who comes to live in and with us. Our Teacher, the Holy Spirit, works to give us knowledge of the world into which we've been spiritually born, the kingdom of God—that wider, eternally *real* world of which we know so little.

Throughout Helen Keller's life she had to practice what her teacher labored to convey to her about the real, physical world and how to live in it. And although Helen never actually saw or heard another human being, she developed numerous deep friendships. She learned to transcend her limitations to interact with the people in her life.

Even with a resident teacher, Helen had to practice what she had been taught. Otherwise she would have flailed and stumbled her way through life. Locked in a prison of dark isolation, Helen would have been unable to share her heart with another. What a tragedy for Helen. What a sorrow for Helen's parents, who yearned to communicate their love and themselves to their beloved child. All of that life-transforming reality was there—all around her. Yet Helen could not have experienced it.

We, too, must continue to practice the reality of Christ's

presence and his kingdom, which the Spirit conveys. This enables us to develop a deep friendship with the Person our humanly limited eyes and ears neither see nor hear. And immeasurably more glorious still, we have the assurance that he whom we see now by faith, we shall see one day by sight.

Obviously the analogy doesn't fit at every point. For instance, I have known intellectually of my heavenly Parent's love for decades. Nevertheless, I feel what I imagine Helen Keller must have felt when she began to experience more fully the reality of a world she had previously groped awkwardly to understand.

Like Helen, I am the cherished child of a loving Father and part of a family in which I have always had a secure place of belonging. And like Helen, I did not truly *experience* that reality until I began to practice what my resident Teacher pressed on me.

In the same way, our heavenly Father wants us to know more than how to practice spiritual habits. He wants us to know him—his faithful heart and his nonabandoning love.

Helen's parents wanted her to know more than just sign language and braille. They wanted her to know *them.* In the same way, our heavenly Father wants us to know more than how to practice spiritual habits. He wants us to know *him*—his faithful heart and his nonabandoning love.

As children and/or adults, some of us have experienced

betrayal of trust, abandonment, and insecurity about our place of belonging in relationships. Therefore, it is within relationships that we can begin to experience trustworthy love and secure belonging. Healthy human relationships with faithful spouses, caring friends, godly counselors, and wise pastors can help. I know because I have had all of them. But we will never experience life-transforming healing from abandonment, the ultimate acceptance we crave, or a rock-solid sense of secure belonging apart from an intimate, heart-to-heart relationship with Jesus Christ, our Immanuel. This, too, I know.

> *But we will never experience life-transforming healing from abandonment, the ultimate acceptance we crave, or a rock-solid sense of secure belonging apart from an intimate, heart-to-heart relationship with Jesus Christ, our Immanuel.*

As I've said, I did not set out to seek relational and emotional transformation. I simply longed to realize God's nearness more fully. But as I spend time focused on and listening to God, he and his promises of faithful love become more and more real. As that process continues, God continues healing wounds of abandonment and satisfying longings too deep to name.

Moving Closer

1. In the past, how have you tried to change?

2. What truths have gotten stuck on the journey from your head to your heart?

3. What can you do to make space in your life to spend time with Jesus to increase the intimacy of your relationship?

4. Ask Jesus to help you experience his real presence and hear him speak to you in Scripture and in silence as you practice *listening* prayer.

5. Don't be discouraged if your first few attempts at listening prayer seem awkward or too silent. Your resident Teacher will slowly open the "ears" of your heart to hear. You may find it helpful, as I did, to keep a notebook to record the words you hear as you listen.

6. Remember that the main goal is to know Christ more intimately solely because of who he *is*—not because of anything we hope he will *do*.

7. Appendix B lists some resources I've found helpful.

Moving On

Like practicing ballet or basketball, the more we practice the presence of God by giving him our full attention, the easier it becomes. And as we do this, we will get to know him more intimately and learn more personally of his faithful love. But there's a catch: Wrong ideas about God create barriers to developing healing intimacy with him.

In chapter 3 we'll see how to break through those barriers.

3 "How Can I Get Close to a God

I Don't Trust?"

A little boy once looked up at the sky and asked his mother, "Is God up there?" After her assurance that he was, the child replied, "Wouldn't it be nice if he would stick his head out and let us see him?"

God did infinitely more than that. Dressed in human flesh, God the Son—Jesus of Nazareth—journeyed this planet for nearly thirty-three years. He wore God's heart on his sleeve. He showed us God's true image in his face.

Jesus sought—among other things—to clarify misunderstandings that would keep us from knowing our Creator, trusting him, and experiencing his life-transforming love. Those misunderstandings are deadly because "we tend by a secret law of the soul to move toward our mental image of God."[1] So to help us get it straight, Jesus said it clearly: "Anyone who has seen me has seen the Father" (John 14:9).

This means that by carefully reading the Gospels to see who Jesus is and what he did, we should be able to develop accurate concepts of God. Right?

If that's all there is to it, then why do so many of us Bible-reading believers struggle with the truth that God loves us as much as he loves others? Or that his promises can be trusted? Or a hundred other things?

I suspect it may have something to do with our earliest theological training.

THE FAMILY SEMINARY

Even if our parents never attended a place of worship, they taught us about God. That's because our parents' daily lives and interactions with us more deeply influenced our spiritual development than any formal religious routines ever could.[2] Just ask Jerry.

Jerry's family-based seminary class included the doctrine that "God doesn't like naughty little boys." For as long as he can remember, Jerry's parents said that to him every time he misbehaved. Jerry told me, "Even after I became a Christian, I never really believed all the Bible verses and the preaching that talked about God's love for sinners. I wanted to—don't get me wrong. I even pretended to. It's just that I never really could. So I worked to obey all the commandments well enough so that God would like me. But I never seemed to be able to do that. So I just worked harder and tried not to think about how angry God must be at me."

Like a lot of us, Jerry had to *earn* a sense of belonging from his parents by not being a naughty little boy. And when that's how we experience acceptance from our parents—the authority figures who are supposed to love us unconditionally—then we usually assume that that's the best we can hope for in *any* relationship, with *any* authority figure.

In contrast, if our parents communicated clearly that we

would always be their cherished child even when our
behavior didn't please them, we learned that we could
trust the people we depended on for care to love us even
if we weren't perfect.

Either way, while we were still kids, God began to wear
the face of our fathers and our mothers. I suspect that's
largely because "spiritual development of God-image is
more of an emotional process than an intellectual one."[3]
It's also a crucial one since our image of God shapes our
spiritual lives.

Even when our families gave us reasonably accurate and
biblical reflections of who God is, as adults we may encounter religious authority figures and institutions that, to one
degree or another, disfigure the face of God. Perhaps it's
that favorite teacher who, we find out, conceals a dark secret
life. Or it could be power-hungry ministry directors who
mock Jesus' servant model of leadership.

Ironically, those of us with perceptions of early abandonment usually feel drawn to exactly those leaders,
churches, and parachurch organizations. We feel so
"at home" there!

"ABANDONING GRACE"

Have you noticed that some supposedly Bible-believing
churches and organizations can be very confusing? They
talk and sing a lot about grace—God's unmerited favor
toward sinners—as the sole basis of right relationship with
him. But the thrust of their teaching pictures a "booster-
rocket" kind of grace.

I know that as a kid I got the clear impression that grace
launched me into my Christian life. But once I was in spiri-

tual orbit, my relationship with God depended more on my righteousness than on Christ's. And my righteousness was determined by how perfectly I followed denominationally determined rules and regulations. Tithing, reading the Bible rigorously, attending church, and avoiding specific sinful activities (e.g., dancing, at that time) became the focus of my spiritual life as a new Christian.

Although I didn't know it then, I was trying to control God's attitude toward me by being good enough to keep my place of belonging in his family. I also didn't know that the booster-rocket concept I was taught gave me a faulty perspective of grace as time-limited and undependable. This unbiblical concept of *abandoning* grace inevitably shifted my spiritual focus from an inward love relationship to outward religious acts—those things I could point to while saying to God, to others, or to myself, "See what I've done? I must be a real Christian."

> *Although I didn't know it then, I was trying to control God's attitude toward me by being good enough to keep my place of belonging in his family.*

The apostle Paul certainly knew about the dangers of an abandoning kind of grace. He confronted the Jewish believers in Galatia about that very issue. And Paul did not mince words in verses 6 and 7 of the first chapter of Galatians. "I am astonished that you are so quickly deserting the one who called you by the grace of Christ and are turning to a different gospel—which is really no gospel at all. Evidently some people are throwing you into confusion and are trying to pervert the gospel of Christ" (NIV).

"Deserting" sounds a lot like abandoning to me. And if we believe God's grace may abandon us, we will abandon God's grace. We'll desert, reject, and abandon grace, and we will substitute perfect keeping of the law as the way to be right (justified) before God. That's exactly what Paul told the Galatians they had done (Gal. 2:16; 3:6-14; 5:1-8).

That's what I did for many years. That's what Tad did, too.

GRAPPLING WITH GRACE

Tad was raised in an abandoning atmosphere both at home and at church. Tad becomes increasingly depressed every year as summer approaches. He once explained the process to me: "As a kid, I hated summer vacation because I never knew where I stood with my parents. However, during the school year I had a solid basis for evaluating my relationship with them. It was either A or B. I mean, school was always easy for me, so I never got a C. My good grades seemed to be awfully important to my parents. You know—a real source of family pride. And I see now that my grades also determined the level of love or approval my parents measured out to me. Naturally I couldn't have explained it to you like this as a kid. But I knew what was going on enough to know I wanted to keep making as many A's as I could. And during the summer I didn't get any report cards."

Tad has a hard time with grace. Oh, he loves the idea. But it makes him feel uneasy. He loses his spiritual footing, so to speak, when he thinks about connecting with God because of what Jesus has done rather than what he can do. For Tad, grace is like summer vacation all year long!

When I was a child, I learned to sing the gospel song "Trust and Obey." And for most of my faith life, I thought the primary challenge was to obey. Well, I've changed my mind. Like the Galatians, many of us may find it easier to trust our own abilities to obey religious laws than to trust God's grace-full, nonabandoning love.

Perhaps faith means, in part, entrusting ourselves to God's promise never to abandon those who abandon themselves to him. And based on our knowledge of God's character and experience of his perfect love, he calls us to obey, not so that he will *love* us more, but so that he can *bless* us more. Make no mistake about it, obedient living brings blessings as surely as disobedient lifestyles produce painful consequences.

> *Perhaps faith means, in part, entrusting ourselves to God's promise never to abandon those who abandon themselves to him.*

Those Galatians misunderstood the truth about God and how to relate to him. Those of us who have experienced rejection and abandonment carry into our faith lives essentially the same spiritual backpack of misunderstandings about God. And what a crippling load it is with its demand for us to look perfect in every area of our spiritual lives!

Eventually that shame-laden baggage becomes too heavy to bear, and we start hiding bigger chunks of our lives. We learn to conceal our most embarrassing flaws and problems so that we don't lose whatever place of belonging we are working to maintain.

While I admit I've never seen it printed in a church bulletin or an organization's newsletter, I know many religious environments in which shame-based expectations clearly conveyed that

> *serious* Christians may have *small* problems,
> and *small* Christians may have *serious* problems,
> but *serious* Christians never have *serious* problems.

This means that if I'm in one of those places, I'll have to hide any of my serious problems if I'm concerned about appearing seriously Christian. And I certainly can't ask for prayer and other help for even the most life-crushing problems. *Especially* not for the most life-crushing problems. I'm not supposed to *have* any.

When was the last time you heard someone stand up in a prayer meeting and say something like, "I desperately need your prayers because I can't seem to stop taking more tranquilizers than I should, no matter how hard I try" or, "Please ask God to guide me to the help I need to break free from pornography's grip on my life"? It's probably been a while—maybe never.

ISOLATED BY SECRET LIVES

What sad irony. The secret keeping we hope will protect us from abandonment in the church actually gives birth to abandonment's twin, isolation from our spiritual brothers and sisters. For

> He who is alone with his sin is utterly alone. It may be that Christians, notwithstanding corporate worship, common prayer, and all their fellowship in service, may still be left to their loneliness. The final break-through to fellowship does not occur because, though they have fellowship with one another as believers and as devout people, they do not have fellowship as the undevout, as sinners. The pious fellowship permits no one to be a sinner. So everyone must conceal his sin from himself and from the fellowship. . . . So we remain alone with our sin, living in lies and hypocrisy. The fact is that we are sinners![4]

Shame and fear powerfully motivate believers' longing for belonging. Like the Galatians and my friend Tad, many of us seem to gain a sense of increased spiritual security when we hide our inner struggles and try to adhere to explicit, external standards. With that approach I can, in effect, give myself a spiritual "performance review" like the ones bosses give their employees. That's how workers know where they stand and what they need to improve to strengthen their places of belonging in a business.

GOD OUR EMPLOYER?

As we're discovering, a secure sense of belonging includes the idea that someone freely chooses to love and value us for who we *really* are. This kind of relating differs dramatically from the interactions we maintain by *earning* someone's approval for what we do. Ideally, we hope to have the former kind of relationship with our parents, spouses, and closest friends. But unless we're totally out of touch with reality, we'll settle for the latter type with our employers.

In that comparison you'll notice two things. First, we have to *qualify* to enter an approval-based relationship. Second, we have to worry about being *disqualified*. Employers may call it laying off, downsizing, or firing, but the result is the same. We're out of that relationship. So we normally try to hide our shortcomings to avoid disqualifying ourselves from our jobs.

Now, here's the problem in our relating to God. Many of us tend to view him more as a demanding employer than as a devoted parent.

As an example, for years at Christmas I heaped tons of extra church activities atop my normally staggering load. (And I secretly gloried when people murmured, "I just don't know how you do it all!") If it weren't so sad, it would almost be funny to compare my religiously related Christmastime frenzy to the seasonally increased workloads at many businesses. At least those employees get Christmas bonuses! Meanwhile, I robbed myself of the joy surrounding the celebration of our Savior's birth.

Why did I do this more Christmases (and Easters) than I'd like to admit? Because I assumed that every time some person at church asked me to do something, God himself was assigning me the task. So with that naive and self-destructive perspective, I could never say no to the overwhelming demands. I felt that they were my divine employer's demands. And I didn't want to damage my relationship with him.

When we relate to God as an employer, we inevitably stumble over the notion of grace. And we miss the life-transforming joy imbedded in the truth that we can do nothing either to qualify or to disqualify ourselves for a relationship with God! We just have to want it and receive it.

Do you know what opens the door for relationship with God? Our need! Or more specifically, recognizing and acknowledging our lack of intimate relationship with him and our desperate need of it. Imagine attempting to get a job on that basis:

> "Sir, I recognize and admit that I don't have an employment relationship with this company and that I desperately need one."
>
> "So, do you have any other qualifications to bring to this relationship?"
>
> "Uh, well, no—not really. Just my need."

Try that little speech the next time you go for a job interview, and see how far it gets you!

And our need *is* desperate. In fact, it is a death-and-life issue. That may not sound quite right. But it is. You see, without Jesus Christ in our lives, we are "dead in trespasses and sins," according to Ephesians 2:1 (KJV). And spiritually dead people can't crank out spiritual life any more than physically dead people can generate physical life.

That truth confronts us with our spiritual helplessness and dependence on God's grace to rescue us from that everlasting abandonment we call hell. It makes us feel like powerless children. And while we may struggle against this view of ourselves, God wants us to come to him as children. Here's why:

> It is as children that God loves us—not because we have deserved his love and not in spite of our undeserving; not because we try and not because we recognize the futility of our trying; but simply because he has chosen to love us. We are children because he is our father; and all our efforts . . . to do good, to speak truth, to understand, are the efforts of children, who for all their precocity, are children still in that before we loved him, he loved us, as children, through Jesus Christ our Lord.[5]

GOD, OUR FAITHFUL FATHER

Christianity stands apart from other religions for one major reason. It claims to speak for a God who personally seeks an intimate love relationship with human beings and spares no expense to make it possible. Sadly, as an abandonment-wounded believer, I'm more apt to see myself as God's employee than as his beloved child.

Making that mental shift from employee to child has been at the heart of my recent spiritual leap. For so long I had depended on externally visible—therefore measurable—religious activities to earn God's "well done, good and productive employee." And I assumed that divine accolades came packaged in the praise of church and ministry leaders.

For years I had held the doctrine of "God the Father" in my head. But it hadn't made it to my heart via that intimate relational route chapter 2 describes. Apparently I follow in a long line of people who've had a similar struggle.

It's difficult for contemporary Christians to grasp the paradigm-shattering impact when Jesus taught his followers to approach God as a personal, loving father. The entire Old Testament includes only fourteen references to God as "Father," and they all depict his unique relationship to the nation of Israel. "But there is no evidence that *anyone* in Judaism addressed God as '*My* Father.' Yet this is precisely what Jesus did in all his prayers. . . . Also Jesus used the Aramaic word 'Abba,' . . . a very familiar form of address, rather like 'Daddy,' a childlike form."[6]

Jesus not only addressed God as Father, he invites us to address God in this shockingly personal and intimate way. How that unprecedented intimacy with God must have scandalized the theologians who heard Jesus teach! After all, our Savior introduced an astounding premise: When we approach God, we can come to him as a child runs to a loving daddy. And if we question God's desire to be intimately related to us, we need only breathe "Abba!" as a reminder of that incomprehensible reality.

*When we approach God,
we can come to him as a child runs
to a loving daddy.*

We don't usually think of being tenderly embraced by kings, warriors, or judges, and Scripture portrays God in all those terms, too. But a faithful, loving daddy—ah, that's a different story. That's a God we could get close to with the assurance that within his family we have a secure place of belonging.

The Holy Spirit of God used the apostle Paul to write most of the New Testament books from which we draw the major elements of evangelical theology. And Paul, that Judaism-steeped Pharisee of the Pharisees, repeatedly taught about our personal, loving Abba God.

We've already seen how Paul worked to move the Galatian Christians from an employer-employee, works-based way of relating to God into a grace-based approach that would foster a response of loving obedience. His efforts included teaching them about their Abba (see Galatians 4:6-7). Paul also teaches believers about our Daddy God in Romans 8:15-16: "For you have not received a spirit of slavery leading to fear again, but you have received a spirit of adoption as sons by which we cry out, 'Abba! Father!' The Spirit Himself bears witness with our spirits that we are children of God" (NASB).

Slaves have always been even lower on the relationship totem pole than employees are. And slaves and employees have vastly different relationships with owners or bosses than children have with their loving fathers. Especially when that Daddy has the capacity for perfect love—a perfect love that can cast out all our fears, as 1 John 4:18 describes. And there's only one Daddy like that.

The Abba of Jesus, our Daddy God, bears no resemblance to an undependable parent, an unloving spouse, an unfaithful confidant, or any other person who may have disappointed, rejected, or abandoned us.

Don't you think it's time for us to let our Abba wear

Jesus' face instead of the face of whoever twisted his image?

It's time to come home to Abba's arms, where you belong.

Come, despite doubts and fears, despite faulty human models of authority.

Come, choosing to trust God's heart of love.

HEARING GOD'S HEART

Trusting is always a choice, whether we're talking about trusting our next-door neighbors or trusting our Creator. Now, here's the dilemma when it comes to trusting God: We don't trust him because we don't know him. And we don't really know him because we don't trust him enough to risk interacting with him personally. Yet that's the only way we'll really get to know God and hear him speak his heart to us. And only then do we learn just how trustworthy he is. (Are you still with me here?) But there's more.

> *We don't trust him because we don't know him. And we don't really know him because we don't trust him enough to risk interacting with him personally.*

Without getting to know God genuinely and intimately, many of us will have to keep *pretending* to love and trust God because we know we're supposed to feel that way. When that's the case, we won't make the most significant step in our spiritual journey: "Love the Lord your God with all your heart, all your soul, all your mind, and all your strength" (Mark 12:30).

We learn to love God by getting to know God. When you stop to think about it, that's how we learn to love anybody. As we come to know God intimately, we will personally experience his love for us. And we can't help but passionately love him in response (see 1 John 4:19).

But we'll never learn that for ourselves unless we know how to know him. So how in the world do we know the unknowable?

KNOWING OUR UNKNOWABLE GOD

In his classic book about the attributes of God, A. W. Tozer masterfully frames our dilemma and its solution.

> The yearning to know What cannot be known, to comprehend the Incomprehensible . . . arises from the image of God in the nature of man. Deep calleth unto deep, and though polluted and landlocked by the mighty disaster theologians call the Fall, the soul senses its origins and longs to return to its Source. How can this be realized? *The answer of the Bible is simply "through Jesus Christ our Lord" . . . although He shows Himself not to reason but to faith and love.* Faith is an organ of knowledge, and love an organ of experience.
>
> That God can be known by the soul in tender personal experience while remaining infinitely aloof from the curious eyes of reason constitutes a paradox best described as darkness to the intellect but sunshine to the heart.[7]

I added emphasis to some of Tozer's words because they say more eloquently than I ever could what I spent most of the last chapter trying to say. The deepest, most life-transforming truth can be known—deeply, transformingly known—only through personal experience in relationship. And God is the highest goal of our deepest knowing.

We get to know God with the "organs" of faith and love as we purposefully make space in our lives to spend time in solitude, cultivating intimacy with Jesus and his Abba. Solitude is not an end in itself. Intimately knowing God is the end. And solitude is not even the means to the end. The Spirit of God is the means. But solitude creates the condition of inner stillness that, when combined with our willing hearts, invites the means to work.

> *Solitude is not an end in itself.*
> *Intimately knowing God is the end.*
> *And solitude is not even the means to the end.*
> *The Spirit of God is the means.*

As the Spirit ministers the reality of Christ's presence to us, we learn to hear God's heart. And we begin to know, trust, and love him more than we ever thought possible. That's how he continues to reveal his heart to me.

GOD'S HEART TOWARD ME

As I draw closer and listen to Abba, I am learning that he is very tender toward those of us who have been spiritually wounded and who fear him in unhealthy and unbiblical

66

ways. Scripture teaches us to have reverential awe, which is usually called *fear* of God. But too often we fear our heavenly Father because we assume he is just like the authority figures who have rejected and hurt us.

He isn't. And he wants us to know that.

So he tells us.

Near the end of a particularly long and meaningful time I spent listening to God's heart, he inaudibly spoke this:

> *Dear Child,*
> *Come.*
>> *Keep coming to these special times alone*
>>> *with me.*
> *Keep seeking to know me and see me*
>> *more fully, more truly.*
> *I long to show my heart to those*
>> *who seek to know me.*
> *It brings me joy to know the joy they will know*
>> *as they experience my love for them.*
> *All this you are learning.*
> *All this you must share with my other children,*
>> *especially with those*
>>> *who have been wounded and*
>>> *who have been taught to fear me.*
> *I love you, Child.*
>> *This, too, you are learning.*
>> *And you have just begun.*

God uses so many ways to teach me more about who he is in the grace space I give him most mornings. As you would expect, God often speaks personally from a passage of Scripture. For example, after reading John 20:24-31 one morning, I meditated on Thomas's unwillingness to believe that Jesus had risen unless he saw proof. I put myself in that upper-room scene. From a shadowed corner, I watched with my imagination as Jesus spoke his words of loving assurance to Thomas and then turned to say them to each disciple: "Peace be with you." In my imagination, I edged closer to Jesus. And then he turned and spoke those words to me. I gasped aloud and thought I would die from delight. (No, I did not "see" his face. I don't look for his face; I listen for his heart.)

This is the holy conversation that followed as I wrote it in my journal that morning:

> *Thank you, Jesus, for meeting your*
> *faithhearted followers*
> *right where they were.*
> *Thank you for doing the same with me.*
> *I love you, Lord.*

After a brief silence, I "heard":

> *Yes.*
> *I know you do.*
> *Your love is precious to me.*
> *You are precious to me.*
> *Learn to rest in the reality of my presence*
> *whether you are faithhearted or strong hearted.*
> *Keep listening to me.*
> *Keep coming to be with me in these*
> *special, quiet times.*

> *That's how you learn to live at all times*
> *in the reality of my presence.*
> *And as you do that, you will experience me*
> *turning to you to speak my words of loving*
> *assurance*
> *to you—personally.*
> *Reach forth the hand of your heart.*
> *Touch me and believe.*

Some of you may be worried that you might not be able to meditate on a biblical scene or listen for Abba's voice because of wandering thoughts and distractions (see Appendix C for some suggestions). Our God is so gracious, so aware of our human limitations, that he even speaks in the midst of distractions. (If he didn't, we would never hear him.)

> *"Reach forth the hand of your heart.*
> *Touch me and believe."*

For example, one morning as I tried to focus on Jesus, I was distracted by lots of things. My husband and I were leaving later that day for a combined family visit and speaking trip. Papers and books I needed to pack cluttered the room. Early-morning construction traffic near our home dented the smooth silence I sought. And a zillion thoughts skittered across my mind. Yet despite all of that, I sensed God's encompassing grace and mercy as he held me and told me he loved me.

I inaudibly "heard" Jesus say that the excitement and love I felt at the thought of being with my grandchildren, the yearning to hold them and kiss them, was only a pale shadow of his love and delight over me and his yearning to hold and kiss me. That morning I haltingly wrote a description of all this, but I had such difficulty believing what I was "hearing," I didn't put it down in the "holy conversation" style I had begun to use. Still, I wrote a prayer thanking Jesus for what he'd just told me:

> *Oh, dear Jesus,*
> *I long to rest in your secure embrace*
> > *moment by moment.*
> *Thank you for letting me come into your real presence,*
> > *despite my shallow love and deep flaws.*
> *Thank you for yearning to hold me*
> > *and enjoy being with me,*
> > > *just as I yearn to hold and be with my grandbabies.*

I sat silently for a few moments and then more clearly "heard" him say:

> **Yes, dear Child,**
> > **remember that as you hold, kiss, and enjoy**
> > > **them.**
> **Remember, too, that you want to do that**
> > **despite the fact that**
> > **they are not perfect.**
> **They sometimes disobey.**
> **They sometimes run away**
> > **when you want to hold them.**
> **They sometimes make messes.**

> *But you love them beyond words.*
> *You long—yes, ache—to hold them.*
> *Remember, my dear one, your love and*
>   *your yearning over them*
>   *are but dim reflections of*
>   *my love and yearning over you.*
> *Remember and believe this.*
> *Then you will rejoice and rest in me.*

Isn't that precious? Right in the midst of my cluttered thoughts and office, the creator of the universe gently used my own imperfect love for my grandchildren to teach me more about himself and his perfect love for me.

Don't you think you could learn to trust and love a God like that?

OUR SEEKING, CALLING GOD

I recently read about a three-year-old named Emily. After hearing from a television news program about the death of a famous person, Emily asked, "Is he going to heaven?" Her mother explained that the man would go if he had asked Jesus to be his Savior. That prompted Emily to ask the same question about every family member she could think of. And then she added, "You know what, Mom? I talked to Jesus on the phone the other day, and I asked him to come into my heart."

"That's great," Mom replied. "But how did you know his number?"

"Oh," Emily said, "he called me!"

He always does.

Why? Because that's his loving, redeeming nature. Also

because God knows that, instead of seeing him in Jesus, we likely see him wearing the face of some human authority figure. Someone who may have rejected us when we messed up and missed the mark of perfection. Someone unkind and untrustworthy. God understands that we won't reach out to seek him if we assume he is like that, too.

But our Abba is *not* like that.

So he seeks and calls us. Each of us. By his Spirit, God calls us to himself as Savior. Then he calls us to abide in him so that we will know more and more of his grace-full, unfailing love.

Moving Closer

1. Do you feel secure in your relationship with God, or do you feel that somehow you have to earn your place in his family? What is the source of your security or insecurity?

2. What thoughts and feelings cause you to distance yourself from God and his people?

3. Do you fear God in healthy (biblical) ways or unhealthy (unbiblical) ways?

4. Do you see God as a demanding boss or a loving Father?

5. Consider doing a word study of the words *grace* and *loving-kindness* in the Bible.

6. If you've never done it before, ask God to make you his child. You can do it now. You might want to pray something like this:

   Dear God, I know that my sin separates me from you. Thank you for sending Jesus to die to bridge that gap. Please forgive me and make me your child. I want you to be my Father forever. Amen.

7. If you are already a Christian but struggle to believe God is as loving and kind as he is holy and just, begin to pray daily (in the words of A. W. Tozer): "Whatever the cost to me in loss of friends or goods or length of days, let me know you as you are, that I may adore you as I should. Through Jesus Christ our Lord. Amen."[8]

8. Keep spending time purposefully listening to God's heart. He will speak to you.

Moving On

In the next chapter we'll see how experiencing the reality of God with us (you and me individually) brings healing to wounds of self-abandonment.

4 "How Can I Find and Accept the Real Me?"

While driving to Palm Springs, actor Kirk Douglas once picked up a hitchhiking sailor. After getting into the car and glancing over at the driver, the young sailor exclaimed, "Hey, do you know who you are?"[1]

A good question, don't you think?

In this chapter we'll see how we have learned to answer that crucial question within relationships with the most important people in our lives. We'll also look at why the self-concepts we developed may have required us to reject core parts of our *real* selves—the selves we were born to be. And we'll learn how we can risk getting honest so we can begin knowing and accepting our real selves just as our Abba God does.

WHATEVER HAPPENED TO THE REAL ME?

As we were growing up, we sometimes realized that our real selves—who we really are—were disappointing and unacceptable to the people we depended on for care and affection. As a result, they could never give us a secure sense of belonging.

Becoming someone other than our real selves was the only option for many of us. So we became what other people wanted or needed us to be. But in the process we began to abandon our real selves. After a while we, in effect, stopped knowing our real selves. Why? To keep from feeling abandoned by the people we hoped would know us best and love us most.

For example, I remember counseling a few years ago with Mark, an exceptionally bright young man from a troubled middle-class family. Speaking softly and reflectively, here's how Mark described his process of abandoning his real self:

"I love my parents, and I think that deep down they love me. It's just that I don't think they ever really knew me, so I'm not too sure. What I enjoyed doing when I was a kid was finding out what made things work. God's creation just amazes me. But I wouldn't have dared tell Mom and Dad that I loved science and math and wanted to do biochemical research someday. They laughed at 'bookworms' in my house.

"But jocks were heroes. So guess which I tried to be? I was pretty good at football and sports in general in high school. And that's what my parents really enjoyed. But I wasn't good enough to get a college scholarship. And since I had slacked off on the studies and skipped the toughest math and science classes, I wasn't scholarship material there either. So I was on my own for college. My dad hadn't gone to college, and he didn't want to help pay for my tuition. I did a couple of years at a junior college and then got married. I talk about finishing someday. But I don't know. I try not to think about it much. It's just that sometimes I wonder what I could have been if I'd had more of a shove toward science."

Mark essentially abandoned his God-given intellectual gifts and interests to maintain his place as a loyal child. That's just one of countless ways we may have learned to abandon parts of our real selves.

And if we didn't have to learn that as children, we've faced that issue to one degree or another as adults. For example, May told me that when she goes out with her boyfriend, she pretends to like adventure movies even though she prefers romantic comedies. "At least I used to prefer comedies," May explained after describing the movie-preference struggle with her boyfriend. "It's been so long since I went to one of those 'chick flicks,' as my boyfriend calls them, I'm not so sure anymore what *I* like. I just know what he wants me to like."

Then there was Jeremy, who thought he knew what he wanted but abandoned it anyway. "I hate myself for always going along with my boss's not-so-subtle hints that I come into the office on weekends. I know my family needs me at home, and that's where I really want to be," Jeremy stated.

Maybe we can't identify with Mark or May or Jeremy, but maybe we use food or other substances to numb legitimate human emotions like anger or sadness because we were taught that "good Christians" or "big boys" never have those unpleasant feelings. Then again, we may simply remain silent or vague on subjects we care about deeply if we are with people whose views differ from ours, especially if we value the people's approval.

Now, it's true that as adults we can choose not to abandon our real selves by abandoning our preferences, values, needs, emotions, and ideas. But it's also true that if we've been practicing self-abandonment for quite a while, we likely don't let ourselves even *know* our real selves anymore. Besides, even if we still do, in situations involving people whose approval we care about, we may feel as helpless as children in insecure families. And the more "grown-down" or helpless we feel, the more likely we are to experience shame.

Abandoning Our Real Selves with Shame and Perfectionism

If you have just robbed a bank, you probably feel guilty—and you should. (I'd worry about you if you *didn't* feel guilty for robbing a bank!) But if you try to hide the fact that you make mistakes, fail to achieve goals, and are in other ways imperfect, you are experiencing shame that is not grounded in biblical truth. True moral guilt is about what we do; unbiblical shame is about who we are. That's because this kind of shame comes from the belief that something is wrong with me that isn't wrong with others. Why do I call this unbiblical shame? Because Scripture clearly says that God sees all of us as utterly and *equally* imperfect—that is, sinful.

> *True moral guilt is about what we do;*
> *unbiblical shame is about who we are.*

I recently read that the organizers of the National Spelling Bee provide a "comfort room" every year at the finals. That's where children who have spelled hundreds of words perfectly can go to cry, throw things, and be comforted when they finally make one mistake. The children forget the hundreds of words they spelled correctly, and they feel like failures for getting one word wrong.[2]

In spelling bees, nothing but perfection is accepted. But life is not a spelling bee. Yet for many of us, that's how it seems. And we've usually had to construct our own "comfort room," a place to soothe ourselves when we feel emotionally abandoned because we have disappointed the most significant people in our lives by not being perfect. No wonder we feel shame, that sense of being *uniquely*, hopelessly flawed, if we believe that we are supposed to be perfect. And no wonder we fear abandonment if we believe that to be acceptable, lovable, or worthwhile, we have to be perfect. True moral guilt leads to an appropriate fear of punishment, but unbiblical shame leads to a crippling fear of abandonment.

Our perfectionism grows out of illusions about our ability to keep ourselves safe from abandonment by being good enough (or *something* enough). We likely learned our perfectionism from our parents, who learned it from theirs. Our parents needed us to look perfect so that they would look perfect. We served as putty, so to speak, to patch the broken places that might allow abandonment fears to ooze into their awareness.

That perfectionism got reinforced in school if our teachers took for granted all we did correctly and focused only on our errors. And too many employers—and even spouses—take that same approach, which only adds to the shame and fear of abandonment we feel when we're not perfect.

Let me suggest a quick way we can spot shame and perfectionism in our lives. Let's honestly ask ourselves—better yet, ask others who know us well—how often we

- deny our human emotions and needs (because we think we should be able to take everything without feeling or needing anything),
- exaggerate our achievements (because we're afraid that just being our real selves isn't good enough to earn acceptance or respect or love),
- excuse or lie about our inadequacies, mistakes, etc. (because we don't think we should have any),
- blame others when things go wrong (because we don't want anyone to notice that our own shortcomings may have contributed to the problem).

Did you find any signs of shame and perfectionism? If so, you're just like me and everyone else who struggles with fear of abandonment and who longs for lasting acceptance. And all of us with these struggles find a way to protect ourselves from the pain of shame and abandonment fears.

SELF-PROTECTIVE STRUCTURES

Remember Bruce, the former ministry leader we met in chapter 1? Bruce experienced shame and abandonment fears as a child because he was unable to save his alcoholic family. As a child, Bruce couldn't have named his feelings and fears. All he knew was that no matter what he did, it never seemed to be good enough. So as an adult, Bruce worked hard to be the best at everything he did in order to protect himself from experiencing any shame or fear of abandonment.

As I see it, Bruce developed a unique self-protective pattern of living, a kind of personality structure to cope with fear of abandonment and feelings of shame. Each of us does. Our self-protective personality structure expresses itself in our spiritual lives, our relationships, our intellects, our emotions, our choices, and our behavior. Despite individual differences, they are apt to look something like this:

Self-Protective Personality Structure in Major Areas of Our Lives

Spiritual:	Sense of shame, alienation, and abandonment
Relational:	Insecure sense of belonging with a deep need to earn a "place"
Rational:	Preponderance of misbeliefs
Emotional:	Sadness and/or anger used to hide fear
Volitional:	Choices made to defend against alienation and/or humiliation
Behavioral:	Unbalanced focus on relationships and/or accomplishments

---

Bruce understands now that the nothing-is-ever-good-enough feeling he developed in childhood came from believing he should have been able to do everything perfectly and control everything that happened around him. He still values doing his best. But he's learning to live sanely—even comfortably most days—with the reality that *his* best isn't always *the* best in every situation.

Bruce would be the first to tell you that he's a long way from living without any self-protective personality structure. Let's look at what an *ideal*, real self might look like. Based on what I understand of Scripture, I think it would look something like this:

Ideal Aspects of Our Real Selves	
Spiritual:	Deep sense of being fully known, freely chosen, and faithfully loved by our Abba God
Relational:	Secure sense of unseverable belonging and ultimate acceptance
Rational:	Increasingly truth-full reasoning as our minds are being renewed
Emotional:	Full range of emotions, usually expressed appropriately
Volitional:	Consistently responsible, biblically informed choices (and their consequences) that we "own"
Behavioral:	Increasingly mature, Christlike actions characterized by genuine convictions and compassion

Did you notice that this chart describes an *ideal*, real self, not a *perfect* self? Let's face it, that wouldn't be a very "real" real self! Words like *usually* and *consistently* leave room for the shortcomings and sins we still exhibit even when we genuinely love God and seek to honor him. And *increasingly* pictures the Christian's lifelong spiritual journey toward being made more like our perfect Savior (see Romans 8:29).

But aren't born-again, washed-in-the-blood-of-the-Lamb Christians supposed to be living victorious lives? Why all this talk about our weaknesses and failures? I concur with Brennan Manning when he says, "Most of [people's] descriptions of the victorious life do not match the reality of my own. Hyperbole, bloated rhetoric, and grandiose testimonies create the impression that once Jesus is acknowledged as Lord, the Christian life becomes a picnic on a green lawn—marriage blossoms into connubial bliss, physical health flourishes, acne disappears, and sinking careers suddenly soar."[3]

In reality, we do not stop being humans when we start being Christians. I once heard a wise seminary professor and counselor say that if Christian leaders fall, they fall not because they forget they are holy but because they forget they are human. And humans are imperfect. The biblical term is *sinful.*

> *In reality, we do not stop being humans when we start being Christians.*

Yes, as God's children, we despise our sins, and we struggle toward more Christlike living. But too many of us also despise our real, struggling selves. And when we do, the defenses we use to conceal our imperfections from others can also keep us from facing and feeling the truth about our real selves. For when we live with shame and fear of abandonment, we relate to ourselves as enemies.

We avoid honest self-examination because we fear the failings and transgressions it would uncover. But unless we're willing to risk getting honest about who we are, we'll never know who we are!

> *But unless we're willing to*
> *risk getting honest about who we are,*
> *we'll never know who we are!*

LEARNING TO ACCEPT GOD'S ACCEPTANCE OF US

How do we learn to know and accept our real selves? Or, as we usually put it in Christian circles, how can we learn to see ourselves as God sees us?

Scores of Bible verses tell us who we are in Christ. For example:

John 1:12 and 1 Peter 2:9 tell us that we are children of God and that we belong to him.

Romans 8:35-39 tells us that God loves us and that *nothing* can separate us from his love.

Ephesians 1:4 tells us that God *chose* us to be his own.

Colossians 2:13-14 tells us that we are forgiven and that Christ already paid the price for our sin.

Romans 5:1 tells us that we have peace with God through our Lord Jesus Christ.

Colossians 1:13 tells us that we have been rescued from the dominion of darkness and brought into the kingdom of God's Son.

If all we needed to do was memorize and meditate on verses like these, most Christians would not have such unbiblical views of themselves. I think this is the head-to-heart struggle we discussed in chapter 2. I believe that experiencing transforming truth *relationally* provides the solution.

In his book *Abba's Child*, Brennan Manning reflects on the core of our identity: "'Who am I?' asked Thomas Merton. And he instantly responded, 'I am one loved by Christ.' This is the foundation of the true self. The indispensable condition for developing and maintaining the awareness of our belovedness is time alone with God. . . . [In solitude] we discover that the truth of our belovedness is really true. Our identity rests in God's relentless tenderness for us revealed in Jesus Christ."[4]

I *know* this is true! For I now experience the reality that my identity rests in the unshakable love of my Abba, to whom I eternally belong. That's why I believe that intimacy with God is the key to transforming misshapen identities and entire lives.

As the innermost core of us—our "spiritual center," so to speak—experiences belonging to God, we can risk getting to know our real selves. We can surrender our attempts to be good enough to merit God's applause. Then we can be captured by the truth that we are bad enough to require God's grace. How ironic: we can be all right with God only when we admit that we are all wrong!

> The Good News means we can stop lying to ourselves. The sweet sound of amazing grace saves us from the necessity of self-deception. . . . Paradoxically, the conviction of personal sinfulness becomes the occasion of encounter with the merciful love of the

redeeming God. . . . In his brokenness, the repentant prodigal knew an intimacy with his father that his sinless, self-righteous brother would never know.[5]

RISKING REALITY ABOUT OURSELVES

We must begin by getting real. I mean really honest about ourselves and the wrong ways we've tried to meet our desperate longing for belonging.

What is the alternative for Christians? We can keep *pretending* to believe we have sinned so we can *pretend* to believe we have been forgiven.

The result? A spiritual life of "pseudo-repentance and pseudo-bliss."[6]

Only when we deeply accept that we are both totally sinful and totally forgiven can we deeply accept God's acceptance. And we must genuinely, personally *experience* that core sense of our Abba's open-armed acceptance if we ever hope to have his perspective on who we are.

> *Only when we deeply accept that we are both totally sinful and totally forgiven can we deeply accept God's acceptance.*

A major part of allowing God to reshape my distorted view of myself is inviting him to give wisdom in the hidden parts of my most inward being. Psalm 51:6 promises he can provide that wisdom: "Behold, You desire truth in the inward parts, and in the hidden parts You will make me to know wisdom" (NKJV). Several years ago when that verse gripped my heart, I began praying, "Lord, please show me myself little by little, as I can bear it."

And he is doing just that.

For me, it seems to work something like this: God brings my experiences of abandonment and rejection to my awareness so I can bring them to him. Many times I need to confess and receive forgiveness. Other times I need to groan, grieve, weep, and receive healing. As I said in chapter 1, God has frequently used wise Christian sisters and brothers to guide and support me when I needed to face and feel some particularly painful parts of myself and my personal history.

Through this ongoing process, I am learning to praise our awesome Savior God, who has always known what I'm still discovering about myself. And he has loved me anyway! Experiencing our Abba's "anyway love" irresistibly woos me into his presence so that he can tell me more of what I need to hear.

LETTING GOD TELL US WHO WE ARE

"Ask Jesus how he sees you," said the leader of a spiritual-growth seminar I attended last year. Later, alone in my room, I committed the entire exercise to God. Then I pulled an empty chair close to me and imagined Jesus sitting there. I sat silently, surprised at my wildly beating heart.

After several moments I said aloud, "Jesus, please speak to my heart and tell me how you really see me. I'm sorry I feel afraid as I ask because your Word tells me you love those who have trusted in you. Thank you, Jesus."

This is what I wrote as I began to "hear" with the ears of my heart:

> *Dear Child of mine,*
> *I have always loved you.*
> *From the moment you entered your mother's*
> > *womb*
> > *you have been awash in my love.*
> *Even when you felt most unlovable,*
> > *I loved you.*
> *I love you still, Child.*
> > *You can rest in my love.*
> > *You can serve from my love*
> > *You can love with my love.*
> *I will love you forever because you are mine.*
> > *You are my precious possession,*
> > *purchased with*
> > *the blood of my Son.*
> *Yes, Child, you belong to me.*
> *I am your Abba, who knows you and chose*
> > *you.*
> *Live in the peace and joy of my love.*

Wouldn't you think that after receiving such a precious love letter from my Abba, I would never struggle with insecurity and fear of disapproval again? How I wish that were true.

Here's another journal entry that clearly depicts my ongoing, upstream swim against the undercurrent of abandonment. About three months after the seminar experience, I wrote during my morning time:

> *The devotional guide [I was studying] suggested confessing our worst fears. I confessed my fear of not being whatever enough (socially skilled enough, youthful and attractive enough, intelligent enough, educated enough, spiritual enough) to be loved and accepted in particular situations. But then I realized (with wisdom from above) that behind that fear was the fear that Jesus' presence and friendship and companionship wouldn't be enough for me to feel accepted and loved.*

Almost immediately I "heard" this:

> **Dear Child, you are securely, eternally connected to me.**
>> **You are fully accepted, fully loved.**
> **Nothing will change that.**
>> **Nothing.**
> **In some settings you will not be and feel accepted, approved, appreciated—or loved.**
> **Learn to enter more deeply into the reality of my acceptance and love so that you can tolerate more contentedly the discomfort of being left out and criticized.**
> **I AM more than enough, Child.**
>> **Rest and be refreshed by that truth.**
>> **And live it today.**

God proves to be so faithful and patient as I take baby steps toward greater self-awareness and honesty. For instance, late one night a month ago, I was on a plane heading home after speaking at a conference. I was thoroughly exhausted. On my side of my conversation with God, I wrote:

> *Oh, Jesus, draw me and hold me close.*
> > *You know how much I love You,*
> > *and yet how easily my heart and will*
> > *are distracted by silly, flashy, empty "things"—*
> > *wasted hours, needless purchases,*
> > *self-serving projects.*
> > *What folly!*
> *I see myself as so heartbreakingly small,*
> > *self-absorbed, sin-adapted.*
> *I scare myself with the "me-ness" in*
> > *all I think, desire, and do.*
> *Oh, blessed Savior, purify my motives.*
> > *Deepen my hunger to know you—*
> > *to know you more intimately,*
> > *more really.*
> *And please satisfy that deepening hunger*
> > *even as it grows ever more intense.*

Right there, as I slumped in my aisle seat on that noisy Delta jet, Abba said:

> **Yes, Child, yes.**
> > **Come away and come inside to that**
> > **quieter place within, where you can**
> > **hear my voice above those noisy**
> > **voices all around you now.**

> *I know it's difficult, but you can do it*
> *   as you let yourself experience the*
> *   yearning of your soul to be with me.*
> *Yes, come away to me.*
> *Come. Be with me more purposefully,*
> *   though you are with me eternally.*
> *Rest now. Rest in me.*
> *I love you. You bring me great joy.*
> *   I know it's difficult for you to*
> *   receive that. But it is true.*
> *Receive my love and my joy over you*
> *   with simple gratitude and quietness.*
> *   Let that eternal reality draw you*
> *   ever nearer to me.*

I'm learning that as I listen to Abba's heart toward me, I begin to see myself as he sees me. After all, our identities have been shaped—and misshaped—within close relationship and in dialogue with the most important people in our lives. To have an accurate concept of our real selves, I believe we must be within an intimate relationship and in dialogue with the One who truly knows who we are—the One who created and redeemed us. In effect, we establish that dialogue as we create space in our lives to practice the healing presence of Christ.

You may be thinking that what I wrote in each journal entry really says as much about who *God* is as about who *I* am. But that's the point, isn't it? My growing sense of belonging and belovedness in Christ cannot be separated from my growing intimacy with the person and promises of Christ. I need both to rebuild my shaky identity on a rock-solid foundation.

> *My growing sense of belonging*
> *and belovedness in Christ cannot be*
> *separated from my growing intimacy with*
> *the person and promises of Christ.*

REBUILDING ON SOLID ROCK

Two homes in the area in which Garth and I live have done impressive things with large rocks. One house is built around a huge rock located just outside the front door. In the other house the enormous boulder serves as the main wall in the living room.

In times of solitude with God, I sense inner emptiness being filled. Jesus—the Rock—becomes more and more the solid center of my identity and life. It is as if Christ now forms the main wall of my innermost being. In the past I tried to build my life around Christ. But my "center" seemed pretty squishy and clamorous. It was not a place of strength and stillness. I was certainly not filled with a "deep sense of being fully known, freely chosen and faithfully loved," like that of the ideal, real self. There was precious little "secure sense of unseverable belonging and ultimate acceptance" either.

I think our Abba God wants us to know *whose* we are that we may truly know *who* we are. That seems to be a central part of creating a rock-solid sense of ourselves in Christ. In his letter to the Ephesian Christians, the apostle

Paul describes how our true identity is linked with our place in God's family. Here's how Ephesians 1:4-6 sounds when I personalize the passage by replacing the plural pronouns with singular pronouns:

> *Long ago, even before he made the world, God loved me and chose me in Christ to be holy and without fault in his eyes. His unchanging plan has always been to adopt me into his own family by bringing me to himself through Jesus Christ. And this gave him great pleasure. So I praise God for the wonderful kindness he has poured out on me because I belong to his dearly loved Son.*

Did you notice that God's adoption option brings him great pleasure? Isn't that amazing? I'm not sure which astonishes me more, that my Abba would freely choose to make me his child or that he delights in that choice! Both truths leave me speechless with awe.

Like the man born blind, I can't answer every question or fully explain the changes taking place in me. All I know is that I am no longer afraid to take down my self-protective inner defenses and get to know myself—my real self (little by little as God knows I can bear me!).

Perhaps Ephesians 2:12-13 captures best for me how my belonging in God's family transforms every aspect of identity and life. "In those days you were living apart from Christ. You were excluded from God's people . . . and you did not know the promises God had made to them. You lived in this world without God and without hope. But now you belong to Christ Jesus. Though you once were far away from God, now you have been brought near to him because of the blood of Christ."

What an incredible change for spiritual outsiders who once felt estranged from God because of their sins but who now realize that they are loved by God because of Christ's death. They didn't belong to Abba before, but now they belong to him eternally. God promises that very same identity transplant to all who come to him through Jesus Christ.

> *All I know is that I am*
> *no longer afraid to take down my*
> *self-protective inner defenses and get to*
> *know myself—my real self.*

TRANSPLANTED TO ABBA'S LOVE

Since I'm not much of a gardener, plants are safer in someone else's care. In fact, it's a family joke that I have more of a black-and-blue thumb than a green one! However, even I can pick up the gardening imagery in Ephesians 3:17: "I pray that Christ will be more and more at home in your hearts as you trust in him. May your roots go down deep into the soil of God's marvelous love."

As we learned in the last chapter, trusting God is no easy task for those of us with significant abandonment and rejection in our pasts. But as we risk trusting, Christ becomes "more and more at home" in our hearts. What a lovely word picture of increasing intimacy. And as our intimacy with Christ grows, we are gradually transplanted into "the soil of God's marvelous love."

Transplanted from what? From whatever the spiritually barren soil in which we had been originally rooted. That may have been neglect or rejection, betrayal or abandonment. We have been transplanted from wherever we rooted our identities and lives apart from God's marvelous love. That love went to a cross to give us a new core identity as a beloved child of our Abba God.

Theologian and author Henri Nouwen, writing to a close friend, said, "All I want to say to you is, 'You are the Beloved,' and all I hope is that you can hear these words as spoken to you with all the tenderness and force that love can hold. My only desire is to make these words reverberate in every corner of your being—'You are the Beloved.'"[7]

You are the beloved.

You really are!

Oh, I know, I know. You may say that I don't understand you personally and all the awful messes in your life—many of which you've made yourself. That's true.

But God does know. And the reality remains: the forgiven are the beloved.

"But," you may protest, "my worst sins have been after I knew better—after I already trusted Christ as my Savior. I know I won't go to hell. And I can accept that I am forgiven because I've repented. But *beloved?* I just can't imagine that's who I am."

There's a world of difference between knowing we're the *forgiven* and knowing we're the *beloved*. And the sure sense of our beloved belonging ignites our passion to praise and please our Abba. It does not cause us to wink at our sins.

Belovedness at the core of our identities gives us the

courage to risk getting to know our real selves and the loving Father who already does know us. And when we take that risk, we will begin to experience the ultimate acceptance we've always craved.

There's a world of difference between knowing we're the forgiven and knowing we're the beloved.

Moving Closer

1. If you have lost a sense of your real self, how can you begin to rediscover who God created you to be?

2. What self-protective patterns of living have you used to cover your real identity?

3. What parts of the "ideal aspects of our real selves" attract you? What needs to change in your life to move toward that ideal? Ask God to help you make those changes.

4. Ask Jesus to tell you how he sees you. Over a period of several days, as you read Scripture and practice listening prayer, write down what you hear him telling you. (Remember that while God may tell you to change hurtful attitudes and behaviors, he will never tell you that you are worthless or unlovable. But our adversary, Satan, does.)

5. On note cards, write the personalized paraphrase of Ephesians 1:4-6 that appears on page 95. Put the cards where you will see them frequently.

6. As you meditate on your beloved belonging in God's own family, ask him to make that theological certainty your *experienced reality*.

7. If God is bringing painful parts of your life to your awareness, please find a Christian people helper to support and guide you in that difficult process. Don't be ashamed of intense feelings of anger or grief you might uncover. God understands and will help you learn to express them appropriately.

Moving On

In a sense, we must come to the place of belonging to ourselves—our entire, real, unmasked selves. But as we've learned in this chapter, we build self-protective structures that make that impossible until we surrender them to God. Similarly, we develop hiding places we hope will keep us safe in our relationships with others. We'll examine those hiding places and masks next.

5 "How Do I Risk Letting Others

See the Real Me?"

"Who *was* that masked man?"

I'm so old, I remember that question from the *Lone Ranger*—the *radio* program. And to tell you the truth, I have no idea who the masked man *really* was or why he was masked. He was just known as the Lone Ranger.

I think that to some degree all of us gallop into our adult relationships as masked men and women. And the bigger and thicker the masks we hide behind, the more we remain lone *strangers*, longing to be fully known and deeply loved in a secure place of belonging.

If we've been neglected, rejected, betrayed, or abandoned by someone important, we're often afraid to trust anyone deeply again. So we hide behind the masks we hope will protect us from future pain.

Eric, the successful physician we met in chapter 1, hid his relational vulnerability behind the mask of professional accomplishments. Fearing the humiliation of being judged incompetent—which would make him feel unworthy as a person—Eric sacrificed his most important relationships on the altar of personal achievement. Eric said, "It wasn't until I got into counseling after my divorce that I recognized my fear of close relationships. Now I'm trying to learn how to be more aware of my feelings and even risk sharing them. But to tell you the truth, the idea of doing that terrifies me more than any medical school exam ever did."

In contrast to Eric, I think I've spent most of my life hiding behind the mask of people pleasing. I craved close relationships. The closer the better. The thought of risking an important relationship by saying no or by pursuing my own accomplishments struck terror in my heart. In fact, I don't think I ever even considered doing such a thing!

Regardless of how we do it, hiding behind masks seems to make us feel safer—at least until the masks start to slip. Which they eventually do. As hard as Eric tried to be successful, sometimes his self-protective mask slipped, and his colleagues saw the real Eric. And no matter how hard I tried to please people to make them like me, let's face it, not everyone did! Experiences like that usually trigger our shame and abandonment fears anew, which then prompt us to reach again for our masks. Now, that's what I call a *truly* vicious cycle!

Perhaps you noticed that Eric and I hid behind different styles of masks, so to speak. One style seeks approval through pleasing people; the other tries to earn respect through achieving success.

I think each of us weaves our particular mask from individually tailored efforts to please people or to earn respect. One mask does *not* fit all.

HIDING BEHIND DIFFERENT MASKS

Recently I read a study about the styles people use to relate to each other. One group in the study was "preoccupied"

104

with and extremely focused on relationships with others. In contrast with these subjects, who were excessively *other-*reliant, a second group was compulsively *self*-reliant. These people were "dismissing" of relationships and did "not trust that others [would] be there for them and [tended] toward hostility and more distant relationships with others."[1]

Unrelated to either of those studies—in fact, long before I knew about them—I constructed the Mask Style Quiz to help assess our mask styles.[2] Please take the quiz now (see page 106).

And please remember, we *all* hide our longing for belonging and fear of abandonment in one way or another. One style is neither better nor worse than the other. So don't let taking the quiz become an occasion for shame.

Based on your position on the continuum, you will probably identify with either the relaters' or the achievers' style of hiding as summarized in the "Contrasting Mask Styles" chart on page 108.

Exploring Our Ways of Hiding

As I said earlier, when I developed this Mask Style Quiz a decade ago, I didn't know about the study I described above. But I *did* know that most of us seem to choose one of two ways—or more often a combination—to protect ourselves from feeling incompetent and unlovable. That's what Eric and I did.

We all adopt a relational coping style so early in life that we likely have no awareness of ever doing it or of its life-shaping consequences. Our inborn characteristics interacting with our home environment probably pushed us toward the relational coping style we adopted as children. In effect, we used whatever we had in or around us to make ourselves feel as safe as possible. And as adults, we still do that.

Mask Style Quiz

Directions: Circle either the (R) or the (A) based on your perceptions about yourself. Remember that there are no right or wrong answers.

1. It is important for me to be
    - (R) popular
    - (A) successful
2. If I am hard at work on something extremely important and a very distressed friend phones to talk, I will
    - (R) stop what I'm doing and spend as much time talking as my friend desires
    - (A) tell my friend I can't talk at the moment but will get back to him/her
3. It is more important for me to be
    - (R) well liked
    - (A) highly respected
4. It would be worse for me to
    - (R) be rejected by a significant person in my life
    - (A) fail at a significant task
5. It is very important for me to have
    - (R) personal intimacy
    - (A) personal space
6. When it comes to evaluating others, I tend to be
    - (R) naive and gullible
    - (A) suspicious and cynical
7. When it is appropriate to say "I'm sorry," I find it
    - (R) easy
    - (A) difficult
8. It is more important for me to be
    - (R) kind
    - (A) competent
9. In times of conflict with significant people, I feel the urge to
    - (R) stay close to them and try to explain my perspective
    - (A) get away from them as quickly as possible
10. The troubled people I know need to be
    - (R) lifted up and comforted
    - (A) confronted and straightened out

Scoring the Quiz: Count one point for every (A) you circled. Circle that number on the continuum below to indicate your tendency toward what I call the "relater" or the "achiever" style.

R										A
0	1	2	3	4	5	6	7	8	9	10

Before we begin exploring the styles we use to protect ourselves and hide, let me offer a few caveats. First, no quiz can possibly capture all facets of our individuality. As the Scriptures affirm in Psalm 139:14, he has made us "wonderfully complex."

Additionally, let's understand this: *relaters achieve* and *achievers relate*. It's a matter of where we focus that puts us in one category or the other. And our position on the continuum suggests the intensity of that focus. Finally, don't let the title *relaters* mislead you. *Both* self-protective mask styles damage relationships with ourselves, with others, and with God.

If we keep these points in mind, we're ready to take a closer look at the relaters' and achievers' ways of hiding. And an eating disorder metaphor helps me understand the way relaters and achievers hide behind their mask styles.

HIDING BY RELATIONAL "STUFFING"

Seeking relationships is necessary and healthy since we need relationships. Yes, *need*—like food.

Seeking food is necessary and healthy because we were created with a physical requirement for food. God certainly could have made us differently. But he didn't. We were also created with a need for significant human inter-actions—a minimum daily *relational* requirement, if you will. That's because, as we've established in previous chapters, we are more than just physical beings. We are rela-tional.

I think of human interactions as being to our relational natures what food is to our physical selves. We need both. In the past few years we've all heard about eating disorders,

Contrasting Mask Styles

Common Purpose: To avoid experiencing shame and fear of abandonment

Relater's Style	**Achiever's Style**
Worst fears: being unlovable and experiencing alienation	*Worst fears:* being inadequate and experiencing humiliation
Source of safety: relational attachment	*Source of safety:* personal authority
Basic pattern: seeking approval	*Basic pattern:* earning respect
Defined by: personal relationships	*Defined by:* personal accomplishments
Relational attitude: naive, believes everyone is sincere	*Relational attitude:* cynical, questions everyone's motives
In conflict: overcommunicates to avoid being misunderstood; seeks closeness	*In conflict:* withdraws to avoid looking incompetent; seeks distance
Often says: "I'm sorry"; "Are you all right?"	*Often says:* "Who's at fault?"; "You are wrong!"
Seldom says: "No"; "I disagree"	*Seldom says:* "I was wrong"; "I'm sorry"
Dependent on: approval	*Dependent on:* achievement

both compulsive overeating and undereating. So we know that food can be used in lots of unhealthy ways. Just as relationships can.

Relaters have ravenous relational appetites that, in effect, consume others. Yet relaters never seem to feel relationally full. Loneliness always lurks in the shadows. As you can see from the "Contrasting Mask Styles" chart, relaters want to defend themselves against the fear of experiencing alienation and feeling unlovable.

Those of us who relationally "stuff" tend to babble when we are with strangers. The more insecure we feel, the more we overcommunicate, using words to adjust our appearance and improve our impression on those whose approval we seek. And if you're a recovering approval addict like me, you've spent most of your life seeking *everyone's* approval!

All that people pleasing makes perfect sense if we choose to let our personal relationships define us. Essentially that's what Sam and the women we met in chapter 1 did.

For example, Ellen, the pastor's busy wife, looked to other people for a sense of security and personal worth. That's what relaters always do as they gorge themselves on interaction with others.

Here's a little more of Ellen's story. In a discussion about the topic of this book, she told me this: "I don't really get a chance to be lonely, I guess. Being a pastor's wife means I'm busy nearly all the time, working with people on some project, meeting, or activity. But I can relate to the concept of feeling abandoned. Our children are grown and have moved away, you know. To tell the truth, I'm glad that church responsibilities demand most of my time now since they also take up most of my husband's time. I hardly have a minute to myself. But now and then, in quiet moments, I find myself crying and wondering why I feel as if everyone in the world looks past me without seeing. Would you call that loneliness?"

Sounding somewhat confused, Ellen added that last sentence haltingly. Like many of us, Ellen assumes that if she's around lots of people most of the time, she'll never feel lonely. And like too many ministry people and their spouses, Ellen interacts with people continually but has no genuinely intimate friendships. In effect, she's stuffing herself with relational junk food.

Many experts in eating disorders believe that the brain's appetite-control mechanism malfunctions in some self-destructive overeaters. But experts also seem to concur that most overeaters learned to use food to alter their moods. Food makes them feel better.

Of course, any substance or activity that can alter moods has the potential to be used addictively. So overeaters keep eating, and relaters keep relating to others in approval-seeking ways *long after it's healthy to do so.* Why do they do this? For the positive mood change those activities produce. And—as is true with alcoholism or any other addiction—both overeaters and overrelaters ignore the increasingly obvious effects of their "using."

Overeaters are often heard saying things like, "Well, just one more can't hurt." Or, "I didn't want to hurt Aunt Susie's feelings so I had that second piece of pie when she insisted." And relaters are often heard saying things like, "Well, just *one* more major responsibility at church can't hurt." Or, "I didn't want to disappoint Susie so I baked that second pie for the school fund-raiser when she insisted."

Overeaters stuff themselves with food the way relaters stuff themselves with approval-seeking relationships. Yet, too many calories or relationship are never enough to provide the fully satisfying sense of belonging and ultimate acceptance we crave.

HIDING BY RELATIONAL "STARVING"

In stark contrast to overeaters, undereaters seem to fear food because they dedicate themselves to avoiding ever being fat. No matter what. But because they have such distorted body images, no matter how skeletally thin they become, eating remains scary. So they avoid it whenever possible. In the presence of concerned family members or friends, anorexics usually go through the motions of eating by rearranging the food on their plates. They just can't bring themselves to eat, thereby risking weight gain, which they equate with gross obesity.

Anorexics fear loss of control and obesity in particular and food in general. *Achievers* fear inadequacy and humiliation in particular and close relationships in general. And based on the same reasoning, the latter exposes them to the former. So achievers tend to go through the motions of relating. However, they rarely risk actually getting close enough to people to expose serious flaws.

Of course, unless we live in total isolation, we can't avoid human interaction completely. So achievers interact (which feels risky) to accomplish something (which feels safe). As a result, projects take precedence over people.

This is a lot like anorexics' eating celery because they've heard that chewing it burns more calories than it contains.

Achievers love relational distance and are more apt to "bubble" than to babble. By that I mean that they usually enter relationships sealed inside a bubble that allows them to feel safe. They may "float," in effect, through their required interactions, speaking when spoken to. Or if they've learned the value of appearing more relationally involved, they may talk a lot without ever actually revealing anything deeply personal about themselves.

True, they're not going to forge many intimate friendships that way. But then, they're also not going to risk contaminating themselves with more emotional pain, specifically the humiliation that comes from being judged incompetent. So they seek safety in thick, opaque bubbles that don't allow anyone close enough to see personal weakness or incompetence in any area of achievement. That's crucial, since they define themselves by their achievements.

Demotion or job loss can feel like death to achievers, who depend on their accomplishments to protect themselves from feelings of abandonment. George knows that reality only too well.

After nearly thirty years with a large corporation, fifty-two-year-old George has joined the ranks of the downsized. He sacrificed major chunks of his life and his family for his job, and now he is dazed and depressed. He explains his situation like this: "Downsizing, huh? I don't care what fancy word you use for it. I was *canned!* And after all I did for that company for all those years. They just cut me loose. Just like that. I still can't get over it. And I can't seem to pull myself together these days. My wife and kids are worried about me, I know. I guess I should follow through on the company's offer of job-placement assistance. But I don't have the energy even to do that. I just feel as if somebody died."

Of course, not all achievers are as extreme as George. For as I said before, we all hide our relational vulnerability behind some combination of these two mask styles.

Eric, the successful physician, and George, the downsized company man, both hide behind the achievers' mask. Both have sacrificed relationships for achievement. And essentially, both are relationally starving themselves.

When anorexic people start to lose weight, concerned people in their lives pressure them to eat more. However, undereaters don't want to risk the obesity they associate with more food, so they usually figure out how to wear clothing that hides their increasingly emaciated bodies. And of course, they try not to let anyone get close enough to see their skeletal frames without all those protective layers.

When achievers grow increasingly focused on personal achievements, spouses may pressure them to spend more energy on the quality of their relationships. Rather than risk that frightening prospect, most achievers layer their interaction with protective maneuvers that create the appearance of closeness. Buying expensive gifts often does the job.

In reality, relaters and achievers both crave *and* fear intimate relationships in the same way that overeaters and undereaters both hunger for and fear food. Yet the misuses of relationships and food take such divergent paths. Relaters and overeaters seem to give way to hunger, while achievers and undereaters surrender to fear. Why the differences?

POSSIBLE GENDER DIFFERENCES

My terms *relaters* and *achievers* essentially seem to parallel what the study I described earlier called "preoccupied" and "dismissing" relational patterns. I found it interesting that the relationally preoccupied group in the study was *primarily female* because the majority of the people the "Mask Style Quiz" identifies as relaters also are female. Not all, of course, but most.

I firmly believe God created males and females with differences that are more than anatomical. I also believe sin twists all those God-given nonphysical distinctions so that both genders suffer. Because our culture typically teaches males to be more interactively take-charge, more personally aggressive, and more emotionally distant than females, many men might be inclined to think a longing for belonging is kids' stuff. Or if the need for personal closeness affects adults at all, it's just a "woman thing." To these men, the idea of acknowledging relational neediness seems weak and "wussy." And that's more than just feminine intuition speaking.

Christian men have begun to speak out about their resistance to admitting personal weaknesses and relational needs. For example, John Courtright and Sid Rogers recognized these struggles in the midst of coping with the effects of their wives' childhood sexual abuse. They write:

> The last thing a man wants in a crisis is to appear needy. We're repulsed by our neediness. We hate to

114

be vulnerable. We can't stand feeling like a failure in anything. Neither do we relish the thought of letting someone know we're hurting. . . .

Keeping up a strong, manly appearance means that we never let anyone behind the veneer to see our needs or our pain. . . .

We are convinced that deep inside most men is a terrible fear of rejection that drives our compulsion to appear as though we never need anything from anyone. We are afraid of our own weakness; even more, we are afraid that if anyone saw our weakness, they would reject us. We are afraid that if we let anyone know we are hurting, that person would gain the upper hand in our relationship. We would conse-quently lose whatever stature we presently have in the relationship.[3]

The struggles these men describe sure sound a lot like achievers' issues, don't they?

Again, it's important for us to understand that gender is only one of *several* factors that push us toward one way of hiding more than the other. And many of us switch or combine hiding styles depending on the situation.

TRUE CONFESSIONS OF A RECOVERING RELATER

I know a lot of Christians who hide behind the achiever's mask. (Remember, we *all* hide behind something to some degree.) For four decades I've been married to an achiever. But I've never been one.

However, I *am* a relater. And I can offer my experience as a person who seeks to let Abba God minister his grace and peace to me in ways that beckon me out of my hiding place into more balanced and biblical ways of relating and living.

A few years ago, God used his Word to give some wisdom in my "hidden part" about the relational stuffing and approval addiction that had dominated my life. Although I had read the Bible through several times in various translations, it was as if someone had inserted John 12:43 into my Bible for the first time. It tore through my heart like a lance! The verse says about the religious leaders of Jesus' day, "They loved the approval of [others] rather than the approval of God" (NASB).

I cried when I read that. You see, I love God. And I genuinely want his approval. But I suddenly saw—for the first time—that I lived the real nitty-gritty interaction of my daily life for the approval of others.

That day began a continuing process of surrendering my relater-style hiding place to God. And as you might expect, that topic has come up more than once in the holy conversations God and I have had most days this past two years.

For example, a few months ago I was tired and generally out of sorts. Not only that, I was confused and angry. You see, I had missed several days of my precious morning times with Jesus. I was angry with myself and confused about why I had let something so important to me slip by. The morning I resumed my conversations with God, he gave me insight about what was happening.

I realized that I had become hesitant to record experiences in my journal. Part of that hesitance came from the fact that people had encouraged me to include some of those personal journal entries in this book about experiencing the reality of God's acceptance.

I also saw that I feared my inclination to perform for the approval of others. I knew that it would tempt me to journal with divided goals: not just for spiritual growth, but also for possible publication, with the self-aggrandizement that might include. I also sensed that our enemy, Satan, was somehow attacking in the midst of this mess.

And if all that weren't enough, I knew that later that day I needed to prepare handouts for seminars I was presenting at a women's conference. It would be my first time to speak in the area where I now live, and all kinds of insecurities bubbled to the surface of my mind. My thoughts went something like, *All the other presenters were at the conference last year, so they know each other and are good friends. They probably won't like me and will think that what I have to say is stupid.* (Real mature, right?) Then as soon as I realized what I was thinking, I berated myself because I "ought to know better than to let myself think like that!"

In desperation, I wrote the following prayer, interrupted by a parenthetical commentary on two lines that startled me after I wrote them:

> *Oh, my dear Abba,*
> *I love you and praise you for all the ways*
> *   you pour grace over me!*
> *I long to love you with an undivided heart, and*
> *   I fear all that would pull my purpose toward me.*
> *Please sort this all out and cause it to work for*
> *   your glory and my good growth.*
> *Solitude and anonymity seem*
> *   so much safer for me and my soul.*
> *I don't trust myself around the approving nods*
> *   of smiling judges.*

*(What a curious phrase. Even now, am I still doing
everything for the life-or-death, thumbs-up-or-
down verdict of others? How appalling!)*

*Oh, blessed Jesus Christ, beloved of your Abba,
have mercy on me, a self-serving sinner
who yearns to want your verdict only.*

Almost instantly, and with unusual clarity and volume, I
"heard" this in my thoughts:

> **Be quiet now and listen, dear confused one.**
> **You are mine. You are beloved.**
> > **And I know your heart toward me.**
> > **Rest in this reality, Child.**
> **I also know your confusion, your fears,**
> > **and your discouragement.**
> **Don't be alarmed or surprised:**
> > **sinners go astray and wander off;**
> > **children often become confused and afraid;**
> > **but the beloved belong at home with me.**
> **Pursue inward growth and intimacy with me in**
> > **the solitude,**
> > > **then entrust the outcome—seen or unseen—**
> > > **to me.**
> **Continue to seek my glory, to want to want**
> > **nothing besides.**
> > **Leave the rest to me, Child.**

After a brief interruption, I returned to my place of
meeting Jesus and heard these final sentences:

> **You do well to guard your heart.**
> > **Trust also in me to guard you from the evil one.**
> **Rest in the reality of your belovedness.**

I share this lengthy journal entry because it speaks not just to a relater's issues. I believe it contains hints about how all of us can move closer to our Abba and farther out from behind our particular masks.

Whichever hiding style we tend to use, we *do* need to guard our hearts and our thought lives. We also need to become aware of what situations trigger our well-practiced hiding. In addition, we *are* wise to recognize that the enemy of our souls, Satan, is always eager to use our brokenness to drive us further into hiding and away from God by keeping us away from times of prayer and repentance.

If we are to drop the masks we use to hide our relational needs, we must come to the place of experiencing the truth that God knows every detail of our struggles. He knows, and because he is our Abba, he continues to beckon us home to his arms.

Nurturing Imagery: "A Weaned Child"

I hope the "stuffing" and "starving" imagery has been helpful to you in understanding your own style of relating. A word picture in Psalm 131:2 offers us a beautiful image of hope as we struggle with the tension of needing and fearing relationships (or food): "I have stilled and quieted my soul; like a weaned child with its mother, like a weaned child is my soul within me" (NIV).

A weaned child in that culture was one who—after many months of being nourished day and night at its mother's breast—was old enough to walk and talk.

> Every time the pain of hunger came, the child enjoyed the powerful combination of having its stomach filled with warm milk while being held in a close, intimate embrace. Messages of love and valuing flowed in the child's spirit while the life-sustaining milk flowed into its body. A child who has experienced love and nourishment develops a sense of security about life. Once he is weaned, he still needs to eat. But he is not frantic about his next meal. . . . Because of the love and nourishment he has received, a weaned child has grown secure.[4]

As we've been discovering, we do not outgrow our need for relationships any more than we outgrow our need for food. And if we have not been nurtured relationally, we won't have the security a weaned child feels. So when our fears about neglect, abandonment, and rejection threaten to overwhelm us, we're likely to retreat to our place of hiding.

But if we learn to listen to the voice of our Abba God, we will hear him inviting us to make *him* our place of safety. For "the eternal God is your refuge, and underneath are the everlasting arms."[5]

Moving Closer

1. With which mask style—relater's or achiever's—do you most identify?

2. Which people or situations seem to trigger your hiding?

3. What would it take to make you feel safe enough to lower your mask a bit?

4. What specific steps can you take to make that happen? Will you take those steps? If not, why not?

Moving On

Everything we're learning about relationally conveyed transforming truth, about who God is and who we are in Christ, and about how to live without hiding behind masks *can* remain simply lecture notes. But we take this truth into the laboratory of life in the next chapter, where we look at how to reach out to others in healthy relationships.

6 "How Can I Be Secure Enough to Reach Out to Others?"

Perhaps the entire history of human relationships can be illustrated by a grimly humorous story originating in the Middle East:

A duck was about to cross the Suez Canal when a scorpion asked for a ride.

"Do you think I'm crazy?" the duck replied. "If I let you get on my back, you will sting me and I'll die."

"Now wait," the scorpion said. "If I'm on your back out in the middle of the water and I kill you, you'll sink and I'll die, too."

After some discussion, the duck saw the scorpion's logic and agreed to carry him across the water.

When they were in the middle of the Suez Canal, the scorpion delivered the fatal sting.

"You fool!" cried the duck. "Now we'll both die! Why did you do it?"

"You forget," answered the scorpion. "It's the *nature* of a scorpion to sting."

It's the nature of human beings to disappoint and hurt and abandon each other to one degree or another. Even when they promise that they won't.

We are sinners, people of the Fall. This means that the only people we have to relate to are disappointing, hurtful, and potentially abandoning people. People just like us!

And this is no small matter. We do not simply *have* relationships. We *are* relational. Relationships don't just *enhance* us. In great measure, they *shape* and *sustain* us.

As human beings we are all weak and willful as well as capable and kind. And just as we look to others to meet our innermost longings, others look to us to meet theirs. This whole relational scene would almost be funny if it were not so painfully tragic.[1] Can you picture it? A world of needy humans, incapable of extending or experiencing unconditional acceptance, trying desperately to wrest from one another what each neither possesses nor can give.

Meanwhile, our Creator stands with outstretched, nail-scarred hands, inviting us to find in him what he alone can

> *Meanwhile, our Creator stands with outstretched, nail-scarred hands, inviting us to find in him what he alone can give: a life-transforming sense of beloved belonging out of which to interact with others.*

give: a life-transforming sense of beloved belonging out of which to interact with others.

In this chapter we'll explore some of the origins and expressions of our relational struggles. Then we will look at how intimacy with Christ can reshape our human interactions.

WHY DON'T MY RELATIONSHIPS SEEM TO WORK OUT AS I HOPED?

If we were to picture our relational selves as a series of concentric circles, a cross section of that picture might look like the diagram below. God is at the core of our relational self, and virtual strangers are at the outermost circumference. Our other relationships fit somewhere between the core and the outer edge.

Cross Section of Our Relational Selves

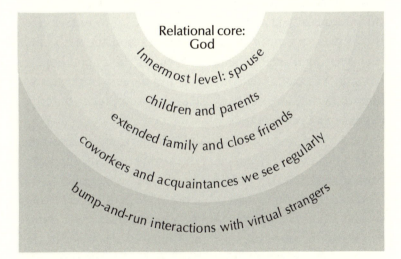

Relational core:
God

Innermost level: spouse

children and parents

extended family and close friends

coworkers and acquaintances we see regularly

bump-and-run interactions with virtual strangers

Even if we grew up with wonderfully healthy models of relating, we all struggle with the impact of sin on human interactions. Sin exerts a centrifugal force that relentlessly pulls us away from our core intimacy with God. It hurls us out to the superficial circumference of our relational lives, out to the shallow bump-and-run interactions, where we can appear self-reliant or compassionate at will because no one gets close enough to know otherwise.

> *Sin exerts a centrifugal force that relentlessly pulls us away from our core intimacy with God.*

The diagram above pictures various levels of relational intimacy, each level requiring a different degree of honesty and vulnerability. Most of us acknowledge that there's no point in trying to fool God about what we think or feel since he already knows us better than we know ourselves. But as we move away from our core relationship with God, each relational level demands less vulnerability and honesty from us. We can, in fact, pretend and defend more successfully the nearer we get to those interactions at the outer edges of our relational lives.

Many of our relational struggles stem from our attempts to find ultimate acceptance at the wrong level of relationship. Forgetting that our core needs can be met only in God, we try to build a secure sense of belonging from the stubble of more shallow interactions. For instance, we may expect to find our desire for emotional intimacy met at the casual acquaintance or friend level, only to be disappointed time after time. It hurts even worse when we fail to find it at the *family* level.

The more insecure we are, the more we will cling to the surface of our hectic lives. Living on the relational edge, so to speak, we work hard to earn approval. And we keep hoping that if we earn *enough* approval, it will magically become (and feel like) love. But since love is a gift we receive, not a reward we earn, that never really works. (Believe me on this.)

Clearly, our individual temperaments also play a role in determining which level of relating feels most comfortable, particularly our tendencies toward introversion or extroversion. For example, a somewhat introverted husband may say, "I don't need any friends. My wife is my best friend." And he may have a difficult time understanding his more extroverted wife's desire for relationships with friends in her Bible study.

All of us must learn to resist sin's centrifugal pull toward shallow interactions. And we're all likely to face some conflicts in even our closest human relationships because of differences in our temperaments. But when we add personal histories of abandonment to the dynamic, our struggles and conflicts intensify a hundredfold.

Cycles of Abandonment and Self-Protection

Relating to others in healthy ways means that we must learn how to love and trust. That's a difficult lesson to master unless we have loving relationships with trustworthy caregivers. When we don't, we may find ourselves trapped in cycles of abandonment where: (1) we *experience* abandonment (real or perceived), so (2) we *expect* abandonment, and as a result (3) *we elicit* abandonment (real or perceived) by hiding behind self-protective masks. Let's see how this looks from the lives of two experts on the subject.

Amy and the Abandonment Cycle

Amy is intelligent, attractive, and unmarried. Amy loves Jesus. Amy is an incest survivor.

> *Relating to others in healthy ways means that we must learn how to love and trust.*

By the time Amy came for counseling, she was heartbroken. She sobbed convulsively as she told me about her sexual relationship with a coworker. "As soon as I met him, I knew I could trust him," Amy said about the man with whom she had been sleeping. (Her comment is a *classic* relater statement.) The "trustworthy" man said he loved Amy and promised that they would marry as soon as he "resolved some personal problems." Amy never pressed him for details because she didn't want him to get angry or think she didn't trust him.

You probably can guess her lover's response when Amy told him she thought she was pregnant and wanted to get married right away. He said he already had a wife and three children, and he wouldn't leave them. Just before Amy quit her job a few weeks later, the man told her she was "way too naive" for her own good. He was right about that—if nothing else.

As it turned out, Amy was not pregnant. So she was not left with a fatherless child. But she certainly was left with a deeper dread of abandonment.

I've counseled many Christian women like Amy who, despite clear convictions about personal purity, began living with men before they married. And I have learned that most of these women have also experienced some form of childhood sexual abuse. That profound abandonment by caregivers they trusted taught these women to believe that the only way they could be close to a man was by being sexually active.

As adults, these women mistook genital union for the intimate, interpersonal connection they craved. Without exception, these women believed that they would hold on to their men with sexual attachment. In effect, they were trying to buy some abandonment insurance with their bodies!

Amy's story represents just one of countless ways we relaters try to protect ourselves from feeling abandoned. The irony is that the very behavior we think will keep us attached only serves to guarantee we *will* feel abandoned. And of course, achievers travel through the same cycle in their own way, as Don knows.

> *The irony is that the very behavior we think will keep us attached only serves to guarantee we will feel abandoned.*

Don and the Abandonment Cycle

I phoned my friend Don several weeks ago to get more of his personal history because he had told me before how difficult it has been for him to learn how to risk getting close to people. Here's some of what Don said: "My parents taught me that it wasn't safe to connect to anyone outside the family. This was reinforced by our hyperseparationist church. At the same time, I learned that it wasn't safe to bond with people *inside* the family and the church either. And since I was pretty introverted by nature, I ended up feeling totally isolated. The only strokes I got were from my performance in school. Eventually I graduated with two master's degrees, one wife, and zero social skills."

Don described throwing himself into his full-time ministry position. Surrounded by people constantly, Don never allowed anyone to break through his impregnable shield of self-reliance. "I never thought about expressing any emotional needs since I had learned long ago that none of them would be taken seriously. Obviously this only undermined my wife's feeble attempts at real intimacy. She had also been pretty wounded in childhood. In fact, it was her decision to get help that eventually led me to join her for some much-needed marriage counseling. Everything in my life seemed to require reevaluation. It was terrifying, the hardest work I've ever done. It still is. But at least I've begun to see some progress."

Don told me that he and his wife are slowly moving toward genuine vulnerability and intimacy. And most days he ministers from a new sense of gratitude for God's nurturing grace rather than from the fear that if he doesn't perform well enough, God will zap him. Don also told me that without consistent effort, he finds himself drifting back into superficial, achievement-oriented relationships that create more isolation.

Like Amy and Don, we all long for true intimacy as much as we fear it. But it doesn't come cheaply. Genuine intimacy never develops without trust. When we trust appropriately, we choose to do so based on other people's record of consistent—but not perfect—reliability. Obviously, this doesn't happen overnight. It takes time to get to know people and to see if they usually keep their promises and are reliable, that is, if they are trustworthy.

However, instead of learning to trust appropriately, extreme relaters and achievers actually trust in self-protective masks to avoid feeling unlovable and alienated or incompetent and humiliated. Of course, when we trust in our relational masks, we inevitably end up feeling even more isolated and abandoned than ever.

In addition, when we relate from behind our well-worn masks, we limit our ability to interact with people in ways that recognize *their* individual needs. That's because we are too busy focusing on our own needs.

Masks Limit Ministry

We can't focus on others' concerns when our own obscure our vision. So we often respond out of our need to protect ourselves rather than out of God's concern for others' needs. What's more, our own relational fears and well-practiced defensive maneuvers often drown out God's quiet voice as he speaks to us about a word or action for a specific person.

How does such a two-sizes-fit-all approach to people work? The last question in the quiz you took in chapter 5 (see page 106) suggests two possibilities. Relaters look at other people and assume they need to be lifted up and comforted. Achievers, on the other hand, often assume that the same people require confrontation and a no-nonsense straightening out.

133

In reality, both approaches are right.

And wrong.

It depends on the individual and the circumstances. The *New American Standard Bible*'s rendering of 1 Thessalonians 5:14 gives us an individually tailored approach to helping others: "And we urge you, . . . admonish the unruly, encourage the fainthearted, help the weak, be patient with all men." We learn from that verse that some people, the "unruly," *do* need to be admonished. But "fainthearted" people need to be encouraged. Still others need "help" if they are weak. However, self-protective masks obstruct our view of others, so we aren't able to see who needs what. This has profound implications for all Christians.

We can't focus on others' concerns when our own obscure our vision. So we often respond out of our need to protect ourselves rather than out of God's concern for others' needs.

One of my Christian counselor friends, Bill, had a rather rude awakening sometime ago. I'll let him explain: "For years, my wife complained that I never used any of my 'counseling skills' when I was relating to her and our kids. And I'd tell her she had the wrong idea about what I did in my office. 'I'm not there to coddle people,' I'd tell her. 'I see my job as showing them where they've strayed from God's Word and getting them to repent and get right.'

"And then my brother was killed by a drunk driver. After

nearly a year of bouncing back and forth between anger and depression, I finally talked to a guy I respect in my field. Don't get me wrong, he said all the correct things. He told me I needed to repent of my hatred of the driver (who escaped with only a few cracked ribs) and to forgive him. He urged me to trust God more and to look for the good he would bring out of this. It's just that I needed him, somewhere along the way, to say it was healthy for me to be grieving. Now I realize that I've taken the same hard-line approach with others for years. Maybe part of the good God is bringing out of all this is that realization."

You've no doubt guessed that Bill is an achiever. On the other hand, as a relater-style counselor, I have missed opportunities to speak some painful truths to people who needed to hear them. I hated to hurt their feelings (and risk their anger).

Genuine interpersonal closeness means we can't keep hiding behind masks of nicety-nice pleasing or self-sufficient performing. And that's a pretty scary thought for a lot of us.

Clearly, healthy relationships don't develop without taking risks and working hard. And marriage magnifies that broad relational reality a millionfold.

SPECIAL CHALLENGES OF MARRIAGE

Unmet longings and fear of abandonment can sabotage marriages in several ways. First, they often display themselves in wildly unrealistic notions of romantic love. Romantic love denies flaws in others. Mature love sees the faults in ourselves and others and learns to love flawed

135

people. Trying to change people inevitably produces resentment. Even when we do it *for their own good.*

Mature love sees the faults in ourselves and others and learns to love flawed people.

Couples who have healthy marriages expect their spouses to change hurtful behavior. They seek help when they're stuck and seemingly unable to change. Still, marital love that lasts over the long haul learns to coexist with a great deal of imperfection.

We will have an extremely difficult time learning to love a flawed spouse if we remain deeply attached to some idealized Prince or Princess Charming who will protect us from ever feeling unlovable or incompetent. We have to make room for spouses' weaknesses, just as we expect them to make room for ours. In our fortieth year of marriage, Garth and I live this reality daily.

Second, in our highly mobile society, we seem to have less and less access to extended families, churches, and neighborhoods as resources for nurturing interactions. Consequently, we often look to our spouses to fill all our deep relational emptiness. And marriages can crumble under this weight of lifelong unmet needs.

Third, this means that everyone who has ever been married has also been disappointed to one degree or another. After all, when we married, we thought we had finally found a person who would make us feel good about ourselves twenty-four hours a day. Then we made the hard discovery that our spouses can't do that for us. What's worse, our spouses often expect us to make *them* feel good about *themselves*.

In fact, this marriage thing has turned out to be a whole lot of hard work! No wonder we're disappointed and discouraged. Many people feel discouraged enough to want to get out. They say to themselves, *I have a right to be happy and fulfilled, don't I? Especially if I had an unhappy childhood!*

> *Marital love that lasts over the long haul learns to coexist with a great deal of imperfection.*

Many of us grew up in an era when our culture taught us that personal happiness was our birthright. And we learned that lesson very well. We bristle at boundaries to our self-fulfillment. Never mind that Scripture teaches that walking with Christ means dying daily. We demand happiness. Now. And for decades, "no-fault" divorce laws have been happy to oblige the fantasy that the solution to a less-than-marvelous marriage involves baling out rather than digging in.

The truth is that nobody has ever had a perfect, problem-free marriage. Nobody has. Nobody will. Can we accept that? Or will we abandon our spouses (and our children along the way) when they fall short of our ideals? Will we opt out when they fail—as they always will—to satisfy all our unmet relational longings?

A HOPEFUL WORD TO PARENTS

Remember Bruce, the guy we heard from in chapters 1 and 4? One of the amazing things about this Christian man is his deep commitment to being the kind of parent who is different from the ones he had.

Sometime ago Bruce told me about the delightful way he affirmed his son and daughter when they were younger. He said that several times a week, he would say to them, "If God lined up all the boys and girls in the entire world—all the children from Europe, Africa, North and South America, and even Australia," then Bruce would pause dramatically and ask, "do you know which little boy and girl I would choose?"

Bruce described how his little girl would smile shyly and duck her head coyly as she said, "I know, Daddy."

He also described how his son would respond with great gusto, "Yep, you'd choose me!"

Bruce told me recently that he's enjoying with his teenage daughter and son a relationship that he never dreamed possible. I'm convinced that his efforts to assure them consistently of their secure place of belonging and his delight in them helped to make that a reality.

As Christians we must come to believe that our heavenly Father has chosen us and set his love on us. And as we are discovering, believing this is not easy for those of us who grew up experiencing mild to traumatic levels of abandonment from caregivers who may have been "there but *not* there" for us. But here's the good news: Even if we had abandoning parents, we can give our children better parents. We will never be perfect. But we can be better, more affirming, affectionate, and trustworthy.

In an earlier book, I described a time decades ago when I was too deeply depressed to care that I was sleeping away my life (sometimes sixteen or eighteen hours a day!). But I did not want to continue sleeping away my two young children's lives. In effect, God used my desire to be a healthier parent to force me to become a healthier person.[2]

Even if we had abandoning parents, we can give our children better parents.

As much as we might want to, we cannot separate the way we parent from the way we relate in the rest of our lives. So, if nothing else can, our love for our children should motivate us to seek more genuinely healthy relationships despite our fears of vulnerability and abandonment.

Happily, we're not left on our own to stumble in the dark searching for a magic key to better interactions.

JESUS' ABBA-CENTERED APPROACH TO HUMAN RELATIONSHIPS

Human relationships have always played an important part in God's plan for his children. For even before sin ruptured Adam's relationship with his Creator, God declared it wasn't good for Adam to be alone. So he gave Adam a woman to be his intimate companion.

Not that all went well in this relationship after the Fall. And because God loves us and knows how sin distorts our relationships, he filled his Word with principles to guide the way we interact with each other.

All the relational guidelines help us immensely. Yet those of us who live downwind of abandonment find the ultimate key to creating healthier relationships in Jesus' Abba-centered approach. I believe our Savior related to people with at least two realities in view.

Reality #1: We Can't Trust People Completely

Human relationships will never be completely satisfying because human beings are never completely trustworthy. The Gospels clearly demonstrate Jesus' compassion for human beings. He even prayed for those who nailed him to a cross! With equal clarity, Scripture tells us that Jesus never put unreserved trust in human beings because—as John 2:24 puts it—"he knew what people were really like." Here are verses 23-25 to provide the context to understand Jesus' perspective on relating to people: "Because of the miraculous signs he did in Jerusalem at the Passover celebration, many people were convinced that he was indeed the Messiah. But Jesus didn't trust them, because he knew what people were really like. No one needed to tell him about human nature."

> *Human relationships will never be completely satisfying because human beings are never completely trustworthy.*

We need someone to tell us the truth about human nature; *Jesus* does not. He witnessed every human betrayal of God and fellow beings from the Garden onward. Jesus fully understood how unstable and untrustworthy human nature is. So he didn't trust himself to people, even when they were convinced he was the Messiah. Jesus knew that the next day they might be convinced he was the devil.

Jesus' perspective on knowing and trusting people stands in sharp contrast to what Psalm 9:10 tells us about knowing and trusting God: "Those who know your name trust in you, for you, O Lord, have never abandoned anyone who searches for you."

In Hebrew culture, a person's name represented one's entire character. So this verse tells us that the more we know God, the more we will trust him never to abandon us. But Jesus knew that we cannot take the same approach with people. No wonder the absolute center verse of the Bible, Psalm 118:8, summarizes those contrasting attitudes toward God and human beings: "It is better to trust the Lord than to put confidence in people."

Throughout Scripture we see the folly of trusting unreservedly in people and the wisdom of trusting in God. Many of us have known this biblical principle to some extent for years. Yet we still often place unrealistic expectations on others to make us feel secure and acceptable. We again face the challenge of getting truth from our heads to our hearts, from theory to experience. And again Jesus' approach provides the help we need.

Reality #2: Dependence on God Helps Us Handle Rejection

I think Jesus related to human beings with a second reality in view: We will transcend rejection only when we have an intimate relationship with our Abba. I draw this from Jesus' overall life and from a passage in the sixteenth chapter of John's Gospel. Listen to part of the dialogue between the disciples and Jesus in verses 30-32: The disciples say to him, "We believe that you came from God." Then Jesus asks, "Do you finally believe? But the time is coming—in fact, it is already here—when you will be scattered, each one going his own way, leaving me alone. Yet I am not alone because the Father is with me."

Do you see it? Jesus' core identity as the beloved Son, his core relationship with his Abba, created a secure sense of being "alone but not alone." This security anchored him through the betrayal, torture, and abandonment he endured.

> *Throughout Scripture we see the folly of trusting unreservedly in people and the wisdom of trusting in God.*

Jesus' perfect intimacy with his Abba provided the experience of unseverable belonging to a degree unique to his position in the Trinity. However, we can follow Jesus' Abba-centered approach. And as we do, our relationships with others will change.

> *We will transcend rejection only when we have an intimate relationship with our Abba.*

How can we tell if our relationships reflect the realities Jesus understood: his own identity and his Father's identity? As our interactions become Abba-centered, we will increasingly

1. reach out to others from a deepening sense of "fullness in Christ" rather than in attempts to get filled;

2. accept the truth that others can never meet all our needs, love us unconditionally, or make up to us in the present what we lacked relationally in the past;
3. recognize that we can't do that for others either;
4. determine to forgive others for their inevitable failings; and
5. determine to acknowledge our inevitable failings and request forgiveness.

Clearly, I'm talking in sweeping relational generalities. And I can almost hear you saying, "Yes, but what about *this* situation?" Countless Christian books provide biblical guidelines for many specific aspects of friendships, marriage, and parenting. These can be enormously helpful.

Yet unless we cultivate an increasingly intimate relationship with Christ in and with us, we will be trying to grasp godly guidelines rather than resting securely in our Abba's arms. It's the difference between an endless chase and an eternal embrace! I learn that startling distinction anew each day.

However, we can follow Jesus'
Abba-centered approach. And as we do, our
relationships with others will change.

LEARNING TO STAY ANCHORED TO ABBA

For decades I've been learning and teaching biblical principles of relating. And while my interactions have grown slightly saner over that time, at the deepest level of my relational self, I lived for many years with fear of abandonment. My intense longing for belonging tended to magnify

the importance of other people's affirmation or criticism.
Especially when it came from those I respected and loved.

Don't let all the past-tense verbs fool you. I still wrestle
with many of those feelings. But not as intensely as before
I began learning how to practice the presence of Christ.
What made the difference? Now I personally experience
belonging to the *person* who is Truth instead of only
believing in *precepts* of truth.

> *It's the difference between an endless
> chase and an eternal embrace!*

I remain absolutely convinced that if we seriously desire
change, knowing and even memorizing biblical relationship principles is essential—*essential* but not *sufficient*. We
need to be anchored in truth at a depth that propositions,
precepts, and principles can't reach. We must be anchored
in transforming truth by an intimate relationship with it.

> *Now I personally experience belonging
> to the person who is Truth instead of only
> believing in precepts of truth.*

Jesus is the tether that anchors me securely to my Abba
at the deepest core of my being. God relentlessly draws
me back to transforming truth when I wander into my
people-pleasing, approval-worshiping ways. It's as if my
craving for relational intimacy is a magnet. I think that's

how God created us. Slowly I am learning to come back to Truth more quickly—to run into his arms, so to speak. But I run not just back to a precept but back to a Person. Not just back to God's Word, but back to God.

> *Jesus is the tether that anchors me securely to my Abba at the deepest core of my being.*

I've discovered that my sin-darkened mind seeks truth far less than my sin-wounded soul pines for belonging. In effect, my hunger for intimacy with God—not some noble quest for theological or relational principles—keeps me teachable and receptive to his truth.

THE ABBA-ANCHORED DIFFERENCE

Recently I've begun to notice inner changes in this area, especially when I am at conferences where I meet lots of strangers. That's the kind of setting that pulls me out to those bump-and-run interactions on the surface of my relational life. I'm learning that those are dangerous for me!

Before I experienced intimacy with God, I spent as little time alone in my hotel room as possible between workshops I gave. Now I spend more time alone with Jesus. I am learning that I need to abide in that relational core with Christ, especially when I'm going to be "performing."

One of the earliest road tests of Abba-anchored relating came last year at a large conference three thousand miles from home. In my hotel room the second morning—after

a somewhat-less-than-perfect first day of "anchored" interaction—I told Jesus, in part:

> *I want to be blind to all*
> > *but your love for me and mine for you.*
> > *And I want to want nothing else. Amen.*

After a few moments of what passes for silence in busy
hotels, Abba God inaudibly whispered this to my heart:

> *Child, keep listening.*
> *I know it is more difficult here with distractions,*
> *noise,*
> > *thoughts of responsibilities pressing in.*
> *Come away to that place of inner quietness with*
> *me.*
> > *Be still.*
> *Listen for my heart, my voice.*
> > *Listen before you speak.*
> *Rest in my love before you share it.*
> *Be here alone with me before you must go there to*
> *be with the crowd.*
> *As you do, you will be filled with my presence, my*
> *peace,*
> > *my liberating love at the core of your being.*
> *Then you can go and speak and minister to the*
> *empty,*
> > *restless, bound ones clinging to the surface of*
> > *their lives.*
> *I long to meet them at the center, too.*
> > *Tell them this.*

I did.

I am.

I'm learning that as I purposefully spend time in the presence of God, he fills me spiritually and relationally. When I do this, I don't hungrily search for others' affirming smiles, nods, or words to feel secure and accepted. And if I fail to do this or if I still feel the sting of "outsiderliness" despite my time with Jesus, I rush back into his presence. That's where the reality of my secure belonging and belovedness comes alive. I don't cultivate anchoring intimacy with Christ in a crowd. It happens in solitude, alone with him.

> *I don't cultivate anchoring
> intimacy with Christ in a crowd.
> It happens in solitude, alone with him.*

Since most of my relating occurs in situations outside of conference settings, God speaks to my daily interactions, too. For example, one morning at home not long ago I poured out my desire for deep transformation in words that pictured my soul as wax. Almost immediately I "heard" God respond:

> *I know you love me, Child.*
>> *I know you want my way in your life.*
> *So let me melt you and crack you open*
>> *so that I might shine through.*
> *Let me melt and break you in the small,*
>> *significant places*

147

that create your days, your life:
with Garth—especially with Garth—
with neighbors, with shop clerks,
with the children and grandchildren
you love so much.
　　They are all children I love so much.
Learn to be quiet.
Learn to yield.
Learn gentleness with others.
Remain teachable, and I will instruct you.
　　Stay close, dear Child.
　　I am guiding.

That's another example of God's teaching me about *painfully practical piety.* After all, the real fruit of intimacy with Christ is not the length of our devotional times but the depth of our God-centered love for others, especially those closest to us.

THE ABBA AFFIRMATION

A few years ago, a friend loaned me a tape by author and speaker Brennan Manning. In it, Manning described counseling an elderly incest survivor who loved and served God but had never really experienced God's love and ultimate acceptance. He told her to spend several minutes several times a day focusing on God. She was to close her eyes and silently say, "Abba," as she inhaled slowly and then, "I belong to you," as she exhaled. Manning said that after this woman spent a few days meditating on the reality that she belonged to Abba, her relationship with God—and her view of herself—was gloriously transformed.

I regularly practice this "Abba Affirmation." It calls me
back to the most important truth about myself: because of
God's grace and love, I belong to him eternally. This is
not some magical incantation to ward off our abandonment anxieties. It is simply one of many ways to reorient
ourselves away from the circumference of our relational
lives and back to the rock-solid center of intimacy with
Christ.

> *It calls me back to the most important
> truth about myself: because of God's grace
> and love, I belong to him eternally.*

With eyes wide open, in the midst of hundreds of
people, I can silently affirm, "Abba, I belong to you."
Alone in the dark stillness of a hotel room, I can whisper,
"Abba, I belong to you." And I am instantly reconnected
with the truth that I am *not* alone or outcast. The King
of kings and Lord of lords has set his love on me and
calls me his beloved. I'm constantly amazed at how this
quiets pounding anxieties triggered by fear of abandonment.

LOVING AS CHRIST LOVES

I must confess that I don't usually seek spiritual and relational wisdom from greeting cards. But that's where I stumbled across this arresting sentence: "Christ has come to us
as love so that we might come to love as Christ."

I believe that we learn to love as Christ does by *experi-*

encing his love, not merely by *studying* his love. And as we spend time practicing the presence of God, we open ourselves to experience the love that transforms both us and our relationships.

> *I believe that we learn to love*
> *as Christ does by experiencing his love,*
> *not merely by studying his love.*

Moving Closer

1. As you look again at the "Cross Section of our Relational Selves" on page 127, which level seems most comfortable to you?

2. Are you spending more time within and closer to the core with Christ than you did a year ago?

3. As you review the five traits of increasingly Abba-anchored relationships listed on page 143, which traits do you see evidenced in your life?

4. What would you need to do to have more Abba-anchored relationships?

5. Are you willing to do it? If not, why not?

Moving On

We can't talk long about reaching out to others without talking about the subject of forgiveness. So that's what we will do next.

7 "How Do I Get Past the Pain, Forgive, and Move On?"

Copper wires hold the larger-than-life-sized body of Jesus—crafted out of twisted sticks and branches—on a twelve-foot cross.

Its creator says it is meant not only to remind parishioners of the suffering of Christ's crucifixion but also to give them "a place to park their pain." During the week leading up to Easter, parishioners scrawl personal sufferings on pieces of yellow paper and nail them to the cross. And, "on Easter Sunday, the holiest day for Christians, congregation members . . . will celebrate the risen Jesus and let go of the pain they nailed to the cross."[1]

Some of us may have parked our pain. (And many of us know exactly *where*, so it's easy to find!) But perhaps we have never nailed our pain to the cross and let it go. In this chapter, we learn that the best place to let go of our pain is in Abba's arms.

We can let go of the pain of rejection, betrayal, and abandonment—even the deep pain of our parents' neglect and abandonment of us. That's usually the most difficult letting go, isn't it? I believe that's because parental rejection pierces us at so deep a level that we can scarcely bear examining it.

THE PAIN OF THE FATHERLESS

How can we ever get past the pain of parental abandonment and move on with our lives? My friend Beverly shares how it happened in her life: "All I wanted from my daddy was a wink. A smile. A pat on the back or a kiss on the top of my head. I wanted his approval. I wanted to make my daddy proud. But I was a miserable failure. He wasn't proud. He didn't even care."

Beverly wrote those words recently to describe some of her early relationship with her father and the pain of his emotional abandonment. In the pages ahead we'll learn more about Beverly and how she is getting past the pain of childhood abandonment, learning to forgive deeply, and finding a new level of personal joy and peace in her life.

Beverly and I—and millions of other women and men—share a common pain: fatherlessness. I never knew my biological father, and the father I thought was mine left without a backward glance. Beverly's father, a traveling salesman, was absent a lot. But what wounded Beverly far more than his being gone from home was his emotional absence when he *was* home. Beverly got little or no attention from her father.

Beverly told me that her younger sister and older brother idolized their father, and he showered them with attention. But somehow Beverly and her dad never connected emotionally. "So I turned to academics to get recognition and to try to make my daddy proud of me," she said. Unfortunately, her father didn't value education.

This is how Beverly describes one of her most painful childhood memories about that: "I had my report card in my hand, attempting to show it to my daddy. He happened to be home at the end of the grading period, and I wanted him to see my report card. I had all A's! And I wanted him to see it and to be proud of me. But he just ignored it. It meant *nothing* to him."

When she recalled this experience during a time of healing prayer a few months ago, Beverly doubled over in pain. "I felt utterly rejected. Worthless," she said, remembering the incident.

By not displaying his love for her, Beverly's dad, in effect, disappeared from her life.

DISAPPEARING DADS

When I talk about the pain of the fatherless, I'm not minimizing the importance of mothers. But moms generally tend to be more emotionally available and physically present to their children. With the high rates of divorce, fathers are a different story. Nearly one in five children

Nearly one in five children living in female-headed households hasn't seen his or her father for five years. Any way you look at it, that's abandonment.

living in female-headed households hasn't seen his or her father for five years. *Five years!*[2] Any way you look at it, that's abandonment.

157

It is no wonder that, as author Robert Bly notes, "father-longing is beginning to replace father-anger. That longing is palpable in maximum-security prisons, as well as in kindergartens, where small boys tend to hold onto the trouser legs of any man who enters."[3]

Dads who disappear—whether emotionally or physically—leave desperate daughters in their wakes. These girls and women are desperate to fill the yearning for a strong, protecting male who affirms their intrinsic worth and loves them with no sexual strings attached. And sons desperately need fathers to model for them what it means to be men. The best mother in the world can't be a father. And both daughters and sons need the strong, solid love of a father as well as the tender, nurturing devotion of a mother.

> *The best mother in the world can't be a father.*

Some of my deepest personal pain has been the father-loss grief I harbored like an emotional abscess for most of my life. Whether or not your father was physically present in your home, many of you know that anguish also.

Several years ago, in a time of intensive counseling with a Christian woman, I finally tapped into that soul-deep pool of pain. As wave after wave of grief and abandonment terror washed over me, I sobbed so convulsively that I had dry heaves. I broke blood vessels under both eyes! As unpleasant as this all sounds, God made that time one of the major milestones in my ongoing healing journey.

"Don't Touch My Boo-Boo!"

Sometimes those of us wounded by father-loss believe that no one can really understand or genuinely care about all the confusion, struggle, and pain created by that gap in our emotional nurturing. God, our perfect and ever-present Father, cares deeply about the struggles of the fatherless. And he wants us to let him comfort us and do his healing work in us.

> *God, our perfect and ever-present Father, cares deeply about the struggles of the fatherless.*

But there's a problem that reminds me of a recent phone conversation I had with one of my twin grandsons. Last month, three-and-a-half-year-old James smashed two fingers in a heavy door at Vacation Bible School. Both fingernails popped off, and he experienced a lot of pain for nearly a week. Two days after his losing battle with the church door, I told James that if I were at his house, I would want to kiss his fingers and make them feel all better. Immediately—and with impassioned urgency—James protested, "No, Mimi! You can't touch my boo-boo!" (Mimi is my special name to my grandchildren. Like Abba, in a way.)

When God the Father says, in effect, let me touch your pain and heal your heart, we fatherless people often reflexively jerk away saying, "No, Abba! You can't touch my boo-boo!" Yet he must if we hope to know healing at any significant level. And we must be persuaded that God is very different from the fathers (and mothers) who smashed our tender child hearts in one way or another. Otherwise we will never yield our pain to Abba's healing touch.

God's heart is tender beyond our imagining to the plight of the fatherless. In Hosea 14:3, the prophet declares that the fatherless find mercy in God. But in a verse I especially love, Psalm 68:5, our Abba God has the psalmist describe him as a "father to the fatherless."

ABBA'S REPARENTING

"Father to the fatherless" sounds a lot like what is called *reparenting*. Often those of us with parental abandonment in our pasts are urged to find relationally healthy people to provide some of what our parents didn't. We could debate the value of this approach, which I suspect may be more wishful thinking than reality. However, I think most of us would agree on this: the truest reparenting we can ever experience comes from our heavenly Parent. That's why we must understand as much as we can how completely different God is from our own parents—even the good ones. And he is *vastly* different from the impaired ones.

The chart on page 161 summarizes the striking contrast between abandoning parents and our nonabandoning Abba. The first three numbers in the left column describe characteristics that are often part of performance-oriented, shame-based families. The last three numbers note some traits common to those who grew up in these families. The right column highlights corresponding differences in God's relationship with those in his family.

Contrasting our faithful God and our impaired parents helps us know that if we bring our pain to Abba, he will never respond as abandoning parents would. But there's

Contrasting Abandoning Parents with Our Faithful Abba God

With Abandoning Parents	**With Our Faithful Abba God**
1. Unrealistic expectations. They can expect a six-year-old to act like a twelve-year-old, or they can act shocked (or take it personally) when a child does not behave or perform perfectly.	*1. Realistic expectations.* God knows our limitations, so he has no unrealistic expectations (Ps. 103:13-14). And Jesus "knew what people were really like" (John 2:24).
2. External focus. A performance orientation to life is modeled by parents and learned by children.	*2. Internal focus.* God consistently focuses on the condition of our hearts (1 Sam. 16:7; Prov. 4:23; Joel 2:13; Mark 7:21-23).
3. Emotional abandonment. Parents often withdraw affection and tenderness by hands-on abuse or because a child disappoints their expectations or because they are incapable of emotional closeness.	*3. Emotional closeness.* God promises he will never abandon his children even if their earthly parents do (Ps. 27:10). And Jesus, our Immanuel—God with us—promises he will not leave us as orphans (John 14:18).
4. Feelings of unbiblical shame. Children of abandoning parents believe that there is something uniquely wrong with them, something that isn't wrong with anyone else.	*4. A sense of worth.* God sees all humans as equally sinful; see, for example, Romans 3:10-12. (The gospel is *so* democratic; it says we're all a mess!)
5. Attempts to earn acceptance. Children of abandoning parents try to earn approval and love by performing and pleasing others. This is a shift from *being* to *doing.*	*5. Free acceptance.* God often tells his children that he relates to them not because of their perfectly pleasing deeds but because of his gracious (unearned) love and mercy (Titus 3:5; Rom. 5:8).
6. Feelings of never being fully accepted. Children of abandoning parents never feel accepted by authority figures (parents, etc.) because nothing is ever quite good enough	*6. Unconditional acceptance.* God fully accepts us in his beloved Son (Eph. 1:6).

another issue that often keeps us from letting God touch our pain. To put it bluntly: he allowed it. That's what one of my friends calls "the pain of the pain."

GOD CARES ABOUT OUR PAIN

The pain is what happened to us. The *pain* of the pain is that God allowed it. What do we do with that? Where do we go? And even if we grudgingly accept that we don't receive a satisfactory answer to the why of injustice and suffering, one gnawing question remains: Does God really care?

> *The pain is what happened to us.*
> *The pain of the pain is that God allowed it.*
> *What do we do with that?*

Not long ago, I read an article written by Philip Yancey. He stated that when he wrote his best-selling book *Disappointment with God,* he studied the entire Bible verse by verse, looking for expressions of disappointment and doubt. He was amazed to find so many. Entire books such as Jeremiah, Habakkuk, and Job focus on that theme, as do more than a third of the psalms. Yancey said the Old Testament writers asked God several haunting questions: "Will God reject forever? Has God forgotten to be merciful? Doesn't God care about the suffering of his children?"

In striking contrast, Yancey observes, the New Testament epistles express very little of this anguish. And, obviously, pain and suffering hadn't ceased. Yet nowhere does Scripture record the first-century Christians asking, "Does God care?"

They did not seem to wonder if he forgot to be merciful. Yancey reflects on this difference. "The reason for the change, I believe, is that Jesus had answered that question for the witnesses who wrote the Epistles. . . . They learned how God felt about suffering by watching Jesus. . . . By no means did Jesus solve the "problem of pain"—he healed only a few in one small corner of the globe—but he did signify an answer to the question—Does God care? . . . Because of Jesus, I can trust that God truly understands my pain. I can trust that I matter to God, and that he cares."[4]

God is entirely, incomprehensibly different from hurtful, abandoning parents. What's more, God cares about our pain more than we can ever fully know. Because he cares so much about us and because he wants us to move beyond our painful pasts, God tells us to forgive.

> *God is entirely,*
> *incomprehensibly different from hurtful,*
> *abandoning parents.*

Letting Go of Pain by Forgiving

Three of the most freeing and most difficult words in any language are *I forgive you.*

They are freeing to hear.

They are difficult to say with sincerity.

Yet sincerely forgiving those who have wounded us frees us perhaps even more than it frees them. After all, the people who neglected or abandoned us may never even know that we forgive them. And even if they do, they may not care!

Beverly's dad never knew that she wanted to forgive him. He died suddenly from a heart attack when she was twelve years old. It was decades later that she first faced God's call to forgive. And Beverly's initial steps toward forgiveness didn't seem to get very far. In fact, several years after she had forgiven her father "in her head," she got a hint that maybe there was more forgiving work to do.

> *Three of the most freeing*
> *and most difficult words in any language*
> *are* I forgive you.

A few months ago a pastoral counselor was leading Beverly in a time of healing prayer. When he asked how she felt about her father at that moment, she replied, "I hate him. If he were to walk through the door, I would want to smack him!"

UNDERSTANDING FORGIVENESS

Clearly, Beverly was learning what forgiveness is *not* as well as what forgiveness *is*. For example, forgiveness is *not* neat and tidy. Many of us bypass forgiveness because we misunderstand what those three powerful *I-forgive-you* words really say.

1. Forgiveness is not saying, "It's no big deal." On the contrary, it's precisely because whatever needs forgiving is a big, painful deal that we need to forgive. Otherwise we could just excuse it. But forgiving is not excusing.

Oh yes, people may have excuses for why they abandoned us emotionally or physically. "He was just not the kind of man who could keep commitments." "She was always insensitive and self-absorbed like her mother." Or even, "Well, you know he was abused when he was a kid, so that's why he became an abuser." Understanding a behavior does not make it acceptable. Or excusable. That's why we need to forgive if we want to get past it.

2. Forgiveness is not saying, "Now everything will be the way it was before." All of us this side of painful childhood experiences have the same longing: we want to be able to live as if it never happened. But it did. And forgiving those who made it happen does not erase the hurtful experience or its consequences in shaping our characters and our lives.

3. Forgiveness is not saying, "I won't ever have to think about it again." Forgiveness doesn't trigger amnesia. Many of us wish it would, I suspect. Genesis 41:51 suggests that forgiveness changes the quality of our painful memories so much that we lose the sting of the pain. In that verse Joseph talks about God making him "forget all [his] troubles and the family of [his] father." Yet we know from later chapters in Genesis that Joseph had not forgotten his family or his brothers' painful treatment. We need to know that we can forgive but *not* forget.

> *We need to know that we can forgive but* not *forget.*

4. Forgiveness is not saying, "Welcome back into every area of my life." Forgiveness becomes even more complicated and difficult than it needs to be when we believe that if we forgive people, we must trust them with no reservations.

Jeff VanVonderen illustrates that false idea: "If you break into my house, steal my money, and spend it, so you can't even pay me back, I can forgive you (cancel the debt you owe me). But it doesn't mean that I'm ready to let you into my house. And I still don't have money for groceries, so my family will have to live with the effects of what you caused, even after you're forgiven."[5]

This means we can genuinely forgive and still set limits with people. For example, one woman I know has parents who insisted on calling her degrading names, ridiculing her, and being generally abusive with their words. And, although she repeatedly asked them to stop, they refused. As a committed Christian, she takes God's exhortation to forgive very seriously. She also takes her responsibilities as a parent very seriously.

> *This means we can genuinely forgive and still set limits with people.*

She told me, "I decided it would be wise to limit the time my children and I spend with my parents. And I don't let the kids visit them if I'm not with them. I can't do anything about how my parents' verbal assaults hurt me as a kid. But I surely can protect my children from them."

5. *Forgiveness is not saying, "Well, that takes care of that."* Typically, forgiveness is a *process* as well as an *event*. That is especially true with deeply painful issues involving our parents or other significant people in our lives. I've discovered that forgiving can be a lot like packaging an octopus.

Just about the time you think you have it all wrapped up, something else pops out!

The "something else" can be new memories of old hurts or emotional storms that erupt as we work through hurtful experiences. And these things can surface even after we've made a commitment to forgive the hurters. This doesn't mean we're failures. It means that forgiving involves an ongoing process of recommitting to our original commitment to forgive.

> *Forgiving involves an ongoing process of recommitting to our original commitment to forgive.*

6. Forgiveness is not saying, "I can do it by myself." None of us can do it by ourselves. I believe that deeply transforming experiences of forgiveness are humanly impossible—without the Spirit of God. Unless God empowers our decision to forgive, we won't stay with the hard work it requires.

What is forgiving? Forgiving is giving up the right to wrong those who've wronged us. It's also refusing to be "overcome by evil," as Romans 12:21 (NIV) exhorts. When we don't forgive, we get stuck in resentment and bitterness. And we miss out on the freedom that forgiving brings.

So why wouldn't we want to forgive people who have neglected or rejected us? Perhaps because, without realizing it, we may be trying to avoid feeling totally abandoned. By nurturing our rage and resentment toward the people who have hurt us, we actually maintain a malevolent attachment to them. And that keeps them a part of our lives. Besides, this crippling connection gives us someone to blame for our character flaws and our problems. To some people, that can seem easier than accepting responsibility to change, which we know will involve a lot of hard work.

> *Forgiving is giving up the right to wrong those who've wronged us.*

Remaining pinned on the barbed wire of bitterness means we continue to miss the reality that *we* are the ones most bloodied, not those we refuse to forgive. As this poem says, we need to release the prisoner:

Release the Prisoner
"Release the Prisoner!
Release or he will die."

Release the Prisoner?
"Where's justice?" my reply.

"Release the prisoner!"
I heard again the cry.

Release the prisoner?
At last I said I'd try.

Release the prisoner—
With Grace my sole supply,

I released the prisoner
and saw that it was I.[6]

Forgiving frees us perhaps even more than it frees those whom we forgive. It's true. I know that personally from working through forgiveness toward my mother, my father, and my stepfather (as well as several friends and one husband from time to time).

In reality, when God tells us to forgive others as he forgives us through Christ, he hands us the key to a richer, freer tomorrow (see Ephesians 4:32). And he will be with us in the process. God empowers our decision to forgive the people who have wounded us. He heals the pain of the wounds, as only he can.

Beverly is living this reality.

> *God empowers our decision to*
> *forgive the people who have wounded us.*

BEVERLY'S HEALING ENCOUNTER WITH GOD

About six months ago, Beverly attended a retreat that became a preamble to her most significant encounter with God. During one of the times of guided prayer, the retreat leader invited the participants to try a classic exercise of surrender to God. He told them to close their eyes and relax, sitting comfortably with their hands in their laps. Then he said something like this: "With your palms down, release to God anything that might be keeping you from having a closer relationship with him."

During the few minutes of silence that followed, Beverly sincerely committed to let go of several situations and relational struggles. But then the leader said: "Now, when you are willing to say yes to God and yes to whatever he has for you, turn your palms up and silently tell him that you surrender to his will."

Beverly began to weep. She sat there for what seemed like hours, unable to turn over her hands. Finally, with an inner wrenching that felt like death, she did. Beverly told me last week that she believes that saying yes to God opened the door to the life-changing inner healing she received a few months later.

Beverly recorded her thoughts about that later experience in her journal and graciously gave me permission to use it. Here are excerpts of what she wrote about her life-changing encounter with God:

"The seminar leader asked me what I would say to my dad if he were standing in front of me. . . . I told my dad how much he had hurt me, that all I ever wanted was to make him proud.

"At that point the leader asked the Holy Spirit to come and to minister his love, comfort, and healing grace to me. Quite abruptly I saw a scene of my high school graduation day. I was at the head of the line as valedictorian of my class. As I was standing there in the line, I had a fantasy that my dad was in the audience, that he caught my eye, winked at me, and told everyone around him that I was his daughter.[7] He was so proud of me because I was the valedictorian. [And she really was.]

"Just as abruptly the scene changed. I was suddenly standing at the *end* of the line. We had been placed numerically in order of our class rank, and I was dead *last* in my graduating class. God as Father approached me there at the end of the line, took off my mortarboard, and sailed it into the air. He then picked me up, twirled me around, and told everyone that I was his beloved daughter.

"I could not contain my joy. It hit me so powerfully that God loves me and is proud of me no matter how intelligent or stupid I may be. He loves me unconditionally. Unreservedly. Immeasurably. He delights in me. I am his. He's willing to tell the world that I am his daughter.

"Even if I were dead last in my graduating class, he loves me anyway.

"Unbelievable!

"Inconceivable!"

Beverly's healing prayer time ended soon after that. But God's ongoing healing process was still underway. Later that evening, alone in her room at the seminar she was attending, Beverly experienced a time of uncontainable delight as she "enjoyed" God as her Father and was aware of him enjoying her as his child.

"But after that joyous 'playtime' with God ended, I was overwhelmed with a sense of grief—of mourning for my daddy. Three distinct thoughts were so pervasive that I found myself audibly saying them over and over. These were the words:

"'I miss you, Daddy. I really do miss you.' [Remember that Beverly's father had died when she was twelve years old.]

"'I'm so glad you're home, Daddy.' [He was a Christian.]

"'I love you, Daddy. I love you so much!'

"In those moments of grieving, I realized that the Holy

Spirit was doing a miraculous work of healing at the core of my being. In the thirty-six-year period since my father's death, I had never been able to say the words *I love you* to him. In fact, it was hard for me to say those words to *any* man—even my husband, at times. . . .

"The dam of bitterness, resentment, hatred had broken. At long last I was able to grieve losing my father—not only losing him through an early death but even more painfully losing him through his emotional absence before he died.

"The next few hours of the night, the Holy Spirit continued the healing process. He brought scene after painful scene of my childhood to my mind, and each time the Spirit was there. In the wee hours of the morning light, God told me that I was to share my experience with other people, that it was 'good news' to be told. I obeyed by sharing it the next morning at the seminar.

"What a wonderful Daddy God had been to me all through my years of growing up deprived of a natural father. God had been there all along. He had never abandoned me. He had always loved and accepted me. He had been there in the painful times, in the joyous times, and in the mundane times. And he is with me still."

God had been there all along.

Beverly surrendered herself to God, saying yes to everything he had for her. And God had for Beverly his gift of freedom from bitterness and a new capacity to love her husband. Is her life perfect and constantly idyllic? Of course not. This is planet Earth. But she says that her new sense of God's fatherly presence and love is transforming her life and all of her relationships. Beverly also knows that she's in a lifelong *process* of being transformed.

Although I've strongly emphasized that changing is a process, that is not the same as saying that we will hurt *forever* as much as we hurt *today*. It is also not the same as saying that we will be dealing with these painful issues forever.

More accurately we can say: "I'll be learning to live in truth each day of my life." Or: "I'll be becoming increasingly free to be honest about myself." And especially: "I'll be experiencing more and more of God's presence and love."

A "BEATITUDE" FOR THE FATHERLESS

God understands how extremely difficult it is for the fatherless to grasp the truth of his goodness and love. He isn't angry about our struggles.

In Matthew 7:9-11, Jesus teaches that God the Father's loving concern for his children far surpasses the concern of responsible human fathers: "You parents—if your children ask for a loaf of bread, do you give them a stone instead? Or if they ask for a fish, do you give them a snake? Of course not! If you sinful people know how to give good gifts to your children, how much more will your heavenly Father give good gifts to those who ask him."

Sadly, many people lack even that *imperfect* model of good fathering to help them connect with the perfect Father in heaven. In John 20:26-29, the disciple Thomas declares, "My Lord and my God" after seeing Jesus' crucifixion wounds. Then Jesus replies, "You believe because you have seen me. *Blessed are those who haven't seen me and believe anyway*" (emphasis added). I realize that Jesus refers here to those who have not seen him in his resurrected body. But in the spirit of what has been called "The Last Beatitude," I wonder if we might find a special word to the fatherless.

If not having seen Jesus in the flesh challenges those who believe in him, how much more difficult is it for those who also have no trustworthy human father? Perhaps there are special blessings awaiting the fatherless as we stumble on toward our Abba's outstretched arms.

Evangelist Charles Spurgeon said: "We cannot always trace God's hand, but we can always trust God's heart."[8] And our heavenly Father's heart is indescribably tender toward the fatherless. We can trust that.

ABBA'S INVITATION

Our Abba God waits for us to allow him to be our Daddy. Today he waits. Each day he waits.

He waits for us to let him love us. He waits for us to let him delight over us. He waits for us to let him touch our boo-boos, those most smashed-up, throbbingly painful parts of us.

Abba, our Daddy God, waits to touch and heal us—to embrace us and whisper his love to us.

In Zephaniah 3:17, God's prophet gives us an unforgettable picture of an awesome Father. A Father strong enough to protect, yet gentle enough to sing joyful songs to his children.

The Lord your God is with you,
he is mighty to save.
He will take great delight in you;
he will quiet you with his love,
he will rejoice over you with singing. [9]

Our Father wants to sing his joyous, comforting love songs over us as he cradles us in his arms. When we practice his presence and learn to listen to his heart, this biblical truth becomes our blessed reality. And as it does, we can release our pain and bitterness to receive the consolation and peace we find only in Abba's arms.

Moving Closer

1. In a time of solitude and silence, sit comfortably with your hands resting in your lap. Turn your palms down as you release to God the pain you may have "parked" in your heart for decades. Ask him to show you his tender heart toward you.

2. If you are sincerely willing, again with palms down, name those who have wounded you with neglect, rejection, betrayal, or abandonment. Tell God you are willing to let him nail their sins against you to the cross where he nailed yours. Name the sins again, followed by a forgiveness statement like, "[Name], I forgive you for [name the sin]." It may be helpful to write out your commitment to forgive. Sign and date it. (God serves as the witness.)

3. If you're not willing yet to forgive those who've hurt you, ask God to make you willing. Or if that's still too much for you to do sincerely, ask him to make you *willing* to be willing.

4. Now turn your palms up if you are willing to say yes to your Abba God and to whatever he has for you.

Moving On

We've looked at how an increasingly intimate relationship with Christ works healing in our relationships with God, with ourselves, and with others.

What more could there be? A lot, really. In addition to some needed reminders, in this last chapter I describe my most powerful and personal encounter with God since I began my journey toward increased intimacy with him. And all I did was show up!

8 "I'm Home Where I Belong."

"Go home where you belong!"

Have you ever heard angry children hurl that command at one another? In this final chapter, I want to echo that directive in a more gentle way by inviting you to join me on this homeward journey to our Abba. And as we go, we'll discover we're not the first generation to live with the yearning to go home to face-to-face intimacy with God. To go home, where we belong.

Hebrews 11:13-14 describes people who were seeking a homeland: "All these faithful ones died without receiving what God had promised them, but they saw it all from a distance and welcomed the promises of God. They agreed that they were no more than foreigners and nomads here on earth. And obviously people who talk like that are looking forward to a country they can call their own."

We know that the Old Testament saints described in that passage experienced rejection, persecution, loneliness. They must have felt alienated and abandoned by those around them. Maybe they even felt that God abandoned them at times. They knew they were not yet home where they belonged.

Neither are we.

Of course, the reality is that as long as we are trapped in these crumbling bodies, we will never know the ultimate face-to-face intimacy that awaits us in heaven with our Savior. Storms of rejection, loneliness, and abandonment continue to buffet us, often throwing us off course. But as we learn to practice his presence in and with us, Abba anchors us in his love, and we begin to experience the acceptance we need and want. I suspect that gives us the best possible preview of paradise.

ABBA'S INVITATION

I spent most of my faith life in churches that gave "invitations," some moments at the end of a worship service allowing people to surrender their hearts and lives to Christ. I want to extend on behalf of our Abba God an invitation to you who *have* asked Jesus into your life but don't see that it's made much difference.

Here it is: Your heavenly Father invites you to come home where you belong. Home to a more intimate, heart-to-heart relationship with him.

I've been wrestling with several dozen competing arguments intended to convince you to begin cultivating intimacy with Christ. And I keep coming back to him. I mean, coming back to what kind of God issues this invitation. Somehow we have to know that if we make that journey home, we'll be welcomed when we arrive.

Not everyone is—by their *human* parents.

I read about two teenage brothers who stole more than

ten thousand dollars from their parents, blowing most of it on everything from compact discs to limousine rides. The parents said that the boys, who were adopted a few years earlier, were no longer welcome at home. "We're just walking around shaking our heads," the father said. "We will not accept them back in the house."[1]

I think that many sincere Christians live in terror of hearing similar words from their heavenly Father. If we actually cry out to our Father, "I want to come home where I belong," what will he say? What will he do?

Our fears and feelings of being left out, of being neglected, of being abandoned lead many of us to live as if we are gardeners or pool attendants who work on the grounds outside a beautiful home. Peeking in the windows, we catch glimpses of the loving acceptance that fills the house. Every time we do, we long to belong to the family that shares such joyous intimacy within those walls. So we just keep trying to behave and work well enough to be invited inside.

The truth is that if we are Christians, we *already* live inside the home. Our Abba has brought us into his family, into his home, where we belong. That's the only place where we'll ever find the ultimate, intimate acceptance we crave.

> *Our Abba has brought us into his family, into his home, where we belong.*

At least that's where Scripture teaches us we live if we are in Christ. But some of us keep living like maids or butlers instead of like real children. Working frantically to earn the right to stay, we never really settle in, kick back, and enjoy our Father's company. In effect, we live in crummy, cramped quarters over the garage rather than in the magnificent main house. And our cell-deep longing for belonging continues to drive us to seek the ultimate acceptance that is ours already as children of our Abba.

Unlike the parents in the newspaper story, our Daddy God never banishes his adopted children from his house. He never walks around shaking his head in shock and disappointment. He already knew all the ways we would try to rip him off, and he still adopted us in Christ into his forever family. And he waits up with the light on when we wander away.

As he often did to clearly convey such an imponderable spiritual truth, Jesus told us a story:

A man had two sons. The younger son told his father, "I want my share of your estate now, instead of waiting until you die." So his father agreed to divide his wealth between his sons.

A few days later this younger son packed all his belongings and took a trip to a distant land, and there he wasted all his money on wild living. About the time his money ran out, a great famine swept over the land, and he began to starve. He persuaded a local farmer to hire him to feed his pigs. The boy became so hungry that even the pods he was feeding the pigs looked good to him. But no one gave him anything.

When he finally came to his senses, he said to himself, "At home even the hired men have food enough to spare, and here I am, dying of hunger! I will go home to my father and say, 'Father, I have sinned against both heaven and you, and I am no longer worthy of being called your son. Please take me on as a hired man.'"

So he returned home to his father. And while he was still a long distance away, his father saw him coming. Filled with love and compassion, he ran to his son, embraced him, and kissed him. His son said to him, "Father, I have sinned against both heaven and you, and I am no longer worthy of being called your son."

But his father said to the servants, "Quick! Bring the finest robe in the house and put it on him. Get a ring for his finger, and sandals for his feet. And kill the calf we have been fattening in the pen. We must celebrate with a feast, for this son of mine was dead and has now returned to life. He was lost, but now he is found." So the party began. (Luke 15:11-24)

COME HOME TO PRODIGAL LOVE

We know this story as the parable of the Prodigal Son. But in some ways that's a misleading title. The term *prodigal* describes someone who is wildly extravagant. And it seems to me that the real prodigal in the story is the *father*, who excessively, lavishly welcomed his wayward son back *home—where he belonged.*

Did you notice that this father seemed to experience as much joy—if not more—because his son chose to come home as the son did because his dad chose to let him? And the father even *ran* to meet his son. That part of the story must have shocked Jesus' listeners because in the first century men as wealthy as this father appeared to be *never* ran in public. It was too undignified. But the father didn't care. His son was coming home! It was time to pull out all the stops.

What a theology lesson! Can you see it? Love has feet: the Spirit pursues. Mercy has arms: our Abba receives us. Grace has a face: Jesus' smile draws us near.

Luke 15:20 tells us that the father felt compassion for his wandering son before the young man ever uttered one repentant syllable. In fact, he was "still a long way off" (NIV). As I pondered this passage of Scripture, I was struck by how that phrase sounded like one in Ephesians 2:13. That's the verse that says: "But now in Christ Jesus you who formerly were far off have been brought near by the blood of Christ" (NASB).

That's one of those biblical truths we memorize far more easily than we live. I'm beginning to *experience* being "brought near" as I draw closer to Jesus in regular times of solitude. In effect, I keep on being brought near. I continue to come back to Jesus. I think maybe that's the secret to living in increasing intimacy with Christ: keep responding to his call to come home.

God has been calling us home to his arms, where we belong, since the Garden.

God has been calling us home to his arms, where we belong, since the Garden. His call fills the far countries and rattles the pigpens. If we dare to believe, we'll hear it. Now, depending on how far the country and how filthy the pigpen when we flee our Father's will, we may have to limp, stagger, or crawl on hands and knees. It doesn't matter how we get there. We need to keep coming back to Jesus.

I did that most dramatically a dozen years ago after some blatantly sinful choices. I still do, as—distracted and discouraged—I meander away from the satisfying center of my Abba's will. Praise God for the restoration that follows repentance when we come home with broken and contrite hearts.

In his book *Ragamuffin Gospel*, Brennan Manning explains that while studying the history of the Christian faith in America's Deep South, he made a fascinating discovery: "Over a hundred years ago . . . a phrase so common in our Christian culture today, *born again*, was seldom or never used. Rather, the phrase used to describe the breakthrough into a personal relationship with Jesus Christ was, 'I was seized by the power of a great affection.'"[2]

God is always more loving and gracious than we would ever dare think.

Make no mistake about it: to be "seized by the power of a great affection" is to be heartbroken by our sinful responses. Nothing will more powerfully pull us to our knees in true repentance than experiencing the great affection of our prodigal Abba. God is always more loving and gracious than we would ever dare think. His mercy and grace scandalize even more than the running father in Jesus' parable.

185

When our sin abounded, his grace abounded much more. When we were far off, he brought us near. And when we later left the home he gave us and headed for a far country, he didn't change the locks on the doors. Oh no. With outstretched heart our Abba eagerly watched for our return. With open arms and extravagant love, he stopped our practiced pleadings and embraced us with the beloved belonging found only in him.

Some of you may protest, pointing to verses like 1 Chronicles 28:9, which use words like *reject:* "And Solomon, my son, get to know the God of your ancestors. Worship and serve him with your whole heart and with a willing mind. For the Lord sees every heart and understands and knows every plan and thought. If you seek him, you will find him. But if you forsake him, he will reject you forever." To be sure, God doesn't drag people kicking and screaming into his kingdom. However, rejection as used in that verse speaks to a person or a nation that steadfastly forsakes God. It does not mean that if we turn from his commands for a time, we will be unable to return because we've been "rejected." We must look to the prodigal father of Luke 15 to hear the heartbeat of God in response to his runaway children.

Many of us abandonment-sensitized people look at such lavish love with clouded vision. We need to ask the Holy Spirit to pour God's love into our hearts, as Romans 5:5 says he will. In fact, the ministry of the Holy Spirit took on a new, richer meaning for me recently as the result of an informal Greek lesson.

Several times in the book of Acts we read that the Spirit "fell" on people (10:44; 11:15). The Greek word that is translated as *fell* in these verses in Acts is the same word that is used in Luke 15:20 for an affectionate embrace. The prodigal father *"fell* on his [son's] neck" (KJV, emphasis added), that is, he "embraced him" (NLT) when his son returned.

The falling of the Holy Spirit is like a divine embrace of love. "When we are embraced by the Spirit, our spirits leap within us, crying 'Abba! Father!' We experience within our heart the amazing love of God."[3]

Amazing love indeed. So amazing—so outside the realm of our experiences with human love—that we have no handles to grasp it. We know performance-based love. But we can barely imagine being *given* love. We're so used to trying to *earn* it. And we're so used to fearing we'll *lose* it. Our loving Abba understands and speaks directly to that fear of losing his love.

COME HOME TO FAITHFUL LOVE

God promises his children a special kind of love relationship. First, he *chooses* to set his love on us just as he did on Israel—for no good reason apart from his loving nature (see Deuteronomy 7:6-7). Then, he declares that he never abandons his children. Even when we turn from his will to ours, God's faithful love pursues us and woos us home. (Is this starting to sound familiar?)

The nation of Israel learned that over and over. About two hundred and fifty times the Old Testament writers used the Hebrew word *hesed* to describe God's loyal, steadfast, covenant-keeping love. Psalm 27 contains a particularly meaningful portrayal of our Abba's steadfast love for those of us with abandonment in our pasts.

Psalm 27:8-10 depicts David's sincere response to God's invitation to seek an intimate relationship. Yet, in the midst of his responsive heart, the psalmist struggles with abandonment fears. Listen to David's plea: "My heart has heard you say, 'Come and talk with me.' And my heart responds, 'Lord, I am coming.' Do not hide yourself from me. Do not reject your servant in anger. . . . Don't leave me now; don't abandon me, O God of my salvation! Even if my father and mother abandon me, the Lord will hold me close."

Like David, we belong to the Savior King, who loves us more than we will ever know. He longs for us to long for him. He invites us to come home where we find belonging in his presence. He invites us to come and spend time with him as excitedly as children with the Daddy they adore. And when we come, we can drop our impressive social contacts and nifty accomplishments on the porch. God wants just our hearts.

He longs for us to long for him.

"AFTER GOD'S OWN HEART"

Have you ever wondered what made David—a man whose life was marked by blatant disobedience and repeated failures—"a man after [God's] own heart" (1 Sam. 13:14)? I believe it was David's unquenchable longing for intimate relationship with his Lord that made him a man after God's heart.

It may have been during the solitude of tending sheep

that David was drawn into intimacy with God. Perhaps in days of praise and nights of meditation the young shepherd learned to trust God's unfailing love. For it seems to me that David—perhaps more than any other biblical character—longed for the presence of God in face-to-face fellowship.

Throughout the Psalms, David repeatedly pleads that God not "hide his face" or be far away from him. David most clearly declares his intense longing for intimacy with God in Psalm 27:4: "The one thing I ask of the Lord—the thing I seek most—is to live in the house of the Lord all the days of my life, delighting in the Lord's perfections and meditating in his Temple."

God's "heart" seeks intimate, face-to-face fellowship with each of us. (God makes that intimate relationship such a high priority—he put on skin and died to regain and secure it when our original parents lost it.) When I seek an intimate relationship with God, I am a person after God's own heart. Just as David was.

> *When I seek an intimate relationship with God, I am a person after God's own heart.*

It's no coincidence that verse 4 (David's desire to live close to God) comes before verse 10 (David's assurance that God will never abandon him) in Psalm 27. David made intimately experiencing God's presence his top priority—the one thing he asked of the Lord. And as David developed a close relationship with God, he experienced

God's holding him close even when he felt abandoned. The reality of God's presence created the reality of God's nonabandoning love.

> *The reality of God's presence created the reality of God's nonabandoning love.*

David had learned to trust God enough to draw near to him. And trusting God requires us to cast ourselves on him even when we don't see him clearly.

I once read a story about a family whose house caught on fire. As they were running out, the youngest boy, terrified and confused, broke away from his parents and ran back upstairs. Moments later he appeared at a smoke-filled window sobbing hysterically.

His dad shouted to him, "Jump, Son! Jump! I'll catch you!"

"But, Daddy," the little boy responded in a panic, "I can't see you."

"Yes, I know," his dad called out. "But I can see you."[4]

COME HOME TO PERSONALIZED LOVE

Does God really see us—you and me—individually? Or does he care only about what we do for him and how well and often we do it? Those of us scarred by performance-based acceptance need to know that if we come home to God's presence, he really sees, knows, and cares about us. Each one of us.

For years I've taught the thrilling theological truth

found in Ephesians 1:4: God chose me to be his child
before the world was created. (No, I can't grasp it either.)
But only a few months into my new walk with him, I experienced the truth that the God who chose me is the God
who knows me. And because God wants me to understand
more about just how well he knows me and how much he
cares about my unique concerns, he arranged circumstances to communicate that to me.

> *The God who chose me is the
> God who knows me.*

Last summer I planned my first one-day silent retreat of
fasting and prayer. My husband was away, and I was able
to reserve a prayer room at a local retreat center run by
German Lutherans. I arrived early in the morning and
was met by a smiling woman garbed in a simple habit.
Somehow I hadn't expected these Lutheran women to
look so—well—nunny.

Because this whole "practicing the presence of God"
enterprise was so new to me, I was still struggling with a
lot of doubts, fears, and misgivings. I desperately wanted to
be right with God and to avoid any heretical extremes. So
by the time my companion and I reached the small chapel,
off of which my room for the day was located, I was more
than a little uneasy.

When I entered the chapel, my anxiety escalated sharply!
In one corner hung a crucifix. Not a nice, suffering-free,
Protestant-approved cross, mind you. A crucifix. When I

expressed my surprise, the sister explained that the found-
ers of their order felt God leading them to emphasize
repentance (that was in Germany during World War II).
The crucifix reminded them continually of the price Jesus
paid for our sins, and that deepened their commitment to
repentance.

As the Lutheran nun prepared to leave me in silence for
the day, she invited me to join the sisters for their late-
afternoon worship service. I accepted, thinking that would
be a meaningful way to conclude the day. I was far more
right about that than I could have imagined at the time!

Hours later, as taped organ music began, the sister
knocked softly and beckoned me into the chapel. She
handed me a piece of folded paper that I saw was an order
of service. I just couldn't see that very clearly since I wasn't
wearing my reading glasses. As I took a seat in the back row
and fumbled to put on my glasses, the introduction to the
opening hymn began. Distrusting my ears, I read the title
of the hymn in the order of service. And I began to weep.

Now, if you had to name a quintessentially Baptistic,
evangelical hymn, a hymn sung frequently with all of its
many stanzas, a hymn you would never expect to hear in a
crucifix-dominated chapel filled with a lot of very nunny-
looking women, what would it be? No, not "Amazing
Grace." You hear that every time the movies or television
want to convey something somewhat Christian. I'm talking
a hymn you'd *never* expect to hear!

As I type this, I'm looking at the bright pink order of
service from that day. I couldn't actually sing much of "Just
As I Am" that afternoon because I was crying. But I can
still hear it in my heart.

Isn't that amazing? Somewhere months earlier in Germany, God moved the heart of some woman to select that particular hymn to begin that day's worship service in all their retreat centers and convents around the world. *That* hymn, which I had sung countless times both at church and in a Billy Graham Crusade choir. *That* day. The day when I cried out to God to show me clearly if I was in his will as I walked an unfamiliar new part of my spiritual pilgrimage. I think God wanted me to know that he was aware of my struggles and that where I walked was not really so new after all. So he tenderly wrapped me in the strains of a familiar old hymn that proclaims his grace and love.

What a touching token of Abba's personalized, individualized love. His attention to the details of my life is light-years beyond my ability to comprehend. But when we come back home where we belong, that's the kind of Father who welcomes us. A Father who longs to draw close to those who long to draw close to him—*just as we are.*

> *His attention to the details of my life is light-years beyond my ability to comprehend.*

SHOWING UP

You may be tempted to think that my experiences of practicing God's presence over the past two years require some spiritual maturity beyond your reach. Nothing could be farther from the truth! I am just like you. Possibly worse.

Please believe this: I have done nothing remarkable. *Nothing.*

I just responded to an overwhelming desire to know
Jesus better, a desire I believe he gave me in the first place.
And then I began spending time with him in order to get
closer to him. In a sense, I just show up—he does the
important stuff.

I encourage you to begin showing up to cultivate an intimate relationship with Christ. We evangelicals have focused
on having a place in our belief systems to "make a decision for
Christ." Don't you think it's time we also care about making
space in our schedules to build a relationship with Christ?

> *I encourage you to begin*
> *showing up to cultivate an intimate*
> *relationship with Christ.*

We don't have to spend two hours in solitude every day
to do this. (I'm sure you're relieved to hear that!) Perhaps
the changes we need to make are more about depth of time
than length. For example, listening to God as well as talking.
Letting the Bible read us, so to speak, instead of only reading
it. As I said in chapter 2, such changes shift the focus from
acquiring information to building relationship. Appendix B
suggests some resources to help you get started.

As we regularly show up to be with God, our relationship
with Christ grows more personal and intimate. And although
it's only a fringe benefit and not the primary goal, I've
discovered that we also begin to experience deep healing in
old wounds of abandonment. At this very moment, we can
let those wounds and our deep unmet longing for belonging
drive us into the arms of our Abba God.

194

God planted the longing for belonging in our hearts so that it might draw us into intimate relationship with him. And he can also use the very worst the world has to throw at us to do the same. Then we will know from personal experience how merciful and loving God is—how he redeems our pain and comforts us to an unimaginable depth. These *blessings* of God will become more real in our lives because we will experience *God* as more real.

> *God planted the longing for belonging in our hearts so that it might draw us into intimate relationship with him.*

When that happens—as it does when we show up regularly—we can point others to our Abba and the reality of his prodigal willingness to call us his beloved. But unless we are *living* this reality, we are like travel agents handing out beautiful brochures about places we've never visited. Sadly, I think that describes too many Christians who believe that we've been called to "fake it for Jesus' sake."

We haven't.

We've been called home.

COME HOME WHERE YOU BELONG

Child of God, come home where you belong!

Now.

Right now tell your Abba you long to draw near to him so that you might know him more intimately. And if you don't feel that longing, ask him to deepen it until it breaks through your fears and into your awareness.

If you've been living in clearly unbiblical ways, you may worry that you won't be able to find God if you seek to move nearer to him. You don't have to "find God," friend. As E. Stanley Jones, that great missionary to India, explained, "I didn't find God—he found me. I turned around in repentance and faith, and I was in his arms."[5]

Don't wait until you have all your behavioral loose ends tied up. You never will.

Just come.

We yearn to behave in better, holier ways. But our primary desire is older and deeper than that. I think we don't long so much to *behave* well enough to *earn* a place of belonging, as to be *loved* well enough to be *given* a place of belonging. God knows that about us. That's why he assures his imperfect offspring that nothing can ever separate us from his love displayed in Christ Jesus our Lord. (If you haven't done it lately, stop and read Romans 8:35-39. And personalize it as you do.)

> *I think we don't long so much to* behave
> *well enough to* earn *a place of belonging, as to be* loved
> *well enough to be* given *a place of belonging.*

I'm going to share one final entry from my prayer journal. It records what I "heard" in response to the outpouring of my heart one particularly miserable morning more than a year ago. I had been practicing the presence of God long enough to begin to see myself more clearly. Any

wonder I was disheartened? What's more, I was trying
frantically to finish what eventually became chapter 4
of this book. Between sobs I pleaded with God to work
deeply in my innermost being and to guide me as I wrote.
After I paused to catch my breath, I heard my heavenly
Father speak this to my heart:

> *My dear child,*
> *Your sorrow, anguish, and tears are the process*
> *and the proof that I am answering your prayer.*
> *Rest in me.*
> *Today, let me hold you quietly in my love and presence.*
> *I AM your Father.*
> *Where else would you go when you're hurt and weary*
> *but home, where you belong, here in my presence?*
> *Learn to listen for my voice*
> *in the stillness and quietness of your heart.*
> *Learn to let my presence nurture and fill you.*
> *Then you will cease striving for what never fulfills*
> *its promise to satisfy.*
> *Come home where you belong, fully, freely;*
> *where you can be loved fully, freely;*
> *where you can find rest fully, freely.*
> *Forever.*
> *Yes, you can tell your brothers and sisters, too,*
> *for I want them to come home where they belong.*
> *Keep doing your part—*
> *"present" your body and mind and heart to me*
> *each day, each moment,*
> *and I will keep doing my part.*
> *I love you more than you can know.*

But as you abide in me—where you belong—
you can know more of my love tomorrow
than you know today.
And eternity has endless tomorrows!

Eternity offers endless tomorrows to experience more of our awesome God and his unfailing love. We will be face-to-face with Truth, who graces us with his presence. We will be forever at peace in the ultimate acceptance of our beloved belonging.

We will be home where we belong.

Home in Abba's arms.

I recommend Peter Lord's *Hearing God* (Baker) as a good starting place for those who are just discovering "listening prayer." It was the first book I read after learning about the contemplative side of Christianity in my friend Gary Moon's *Homesick for Eden*. (Gary also recommends *Hearing God* as a good starting place.)

Peter Lord devotes several chapters to how we can know God's voice and distinguish it from the voice of Satan, our adversary. The following information summarizes some of the author's major points.

Knowing God's Voice by the Approach

1. God calls and woos us with the gentle voice of a shepherd who leads his sheep. Like a ravening wolf, Satan seeks to drive the sheep into panic. He threatens, demands, and intimidates.

2. The Lord's voice is quiet and deeply internal. Satan's voice is intrusive. He is that thief who seeks illegal entrance into the sheepfold that Jesus described in John 10:1.

Knowing God's Voice by the Content

1. God always speaks in ways that concur with major principles of Scripture and his attributes as revealed in Scripture. This is not the same as so-called proof-texting, where a verse is used out of context to make a specific point. That's what Satan did when he quoted Scripture to Jesus during his temptation.

2. God's voice drips with mercy and grace toward us and toward others. He does not condemn our personal worth. God is more apt

to urge us to change our attitudes (and sometimes our specific behaviors). Satan speaks in ways that create feelings of personal condemnation. And he wants us to have condemning, unmerciful attitudes toward others.

3. The Lord's voice usually focuses on changing us rather than on urging us to change others.

4. God's voice is grounded in truth and hope in contrast to being grounded in past, negative experiences. (Remember that Jesus urged his weary disciples to put their nets on the right side of the boat despite their past failure to catch fish.)

5. Our Lord usually focuses on the here and now rather than on the future ("Don't worry about tomorrow" [Matt. 6:34]). Satan encourages us in our natural tendency to live in the past or the future.

6. God's counsel is practical and simple rather than impractical and complicated. For example, Jesus is more apt to tell us to take cookies to a new neighbor today than to take a boatload of Bibles to China next year.

7. Similarly, God usually speaks to the ordinary and mundane in contrast to the spectacular, which appeals to our desire for approval and applause.

Knowing God's Voice by the Effects

1. We will have more hope rather than less when God speaks to us.

2. Hearing God's voice produces more empathy for others. Satan wants us to despise and/or envy others.

3. Listening to God brings a greater sense of peace—even when our outward circumstances do not change. Listening to Satan increases our ingratitude, dissatisfaction, and anxiety.

An Additional Thought about Listening to God

We must be willing to respond to God's inaudible voice with obedient hearts. Listening prayer is not some kind of spiritual "parlor trick" designed for our amazement and amusement. In her classic book, *The Christian's Secret of a Happy Life*, Hannah Whitall Smith says: "Take all your present perplexities then to Jesus. Tell Him you only want to know and obey His voice, and ask Him to make it plain to you. Promise Him that you will obey, whatever it may be. Believe implicitly that He is guiding you according to His word. Surrender all the doubtful things until you have a clearer light. Look and listen for His dear voice continually, and the moment you are sure of it yield an immediate obedience. Trust Him to make you forget the impression if it is not His will" (as quoted in Bob and Michael Benson's *Disciplines for the Inner Life* [Waco, Tex.: Word, 1985], 257).

Here are some of the books that have provided guidance and great blessing on my journey nearer to the heart of God. I've highlighted those I think would be especially helpful if you are just discovering the more contemplative side of your faith life.

Bob Benson and Michael W. Benson, *Disciplines for the Inner Life* (Word)

Joseph S. Carroll, *How to Worship Jesus Christ* (Moody)

Francois Fenelon, *Let Go!* (Whitaker)

Richard J. Foster, *Celebration of Discipline* (HarperSanFrancisco) and *Prayer: Finding the Heart's True Home* (HarperSanFrancisco)

Emilie Griffin, *Clinging: The Experience of Prayer* (HarperCollins)

Julian of Norwich, *Revelations of Divine Love* (Penguin Classics). Sometimes this fourteenth-century classic is titled *Showings.*

Thomas R. Kelly, *A Testament of Devotion* (Harper & Row)

Thomas à Kempis, *The Imitation of Christ,* translated by William Creasy (Mercer University Press). As with most of the ancient classics, there are several other editions by other translators.

Brother Lawrence, *The Practice of the Presence of God* (Spire)

C. S. Lewis, *Readings for Meditation and Reflection,* edited by Walter Hooper (HarperCollins). I love everything Lewis wrote, but I find this collection of brief readings ideal for devotional use.

Peter Lord, *Soul Care* (Baker) and *Hearing God* (Baker)

Brennan Manning, *The Ragamuffin Gospel* (Multnomah) and *Abba's Child* (NavPress)

Gary Moon, *Homesick for Eden* (Servant)

M. Robert Mulholland Jr., *Invitation to a Journey* (InterVarsity)

Henri J. Nouwen, *Out of Solitude* (Ave Maria) and *The Way of the Heart* (Harper & Row). I recommend anything by Nouwen.

Tricia M. Rhodes, *The Soul at Rest: A Journey into Contemplative Prayer* (Bethany)

Douglas Rumford, *SoulShaping: Taking Care of Your Spiritual Life through Godly Disciplines* (Tyndale)

Siang-Yang Tan and Douglas Gregg, *Disciplines of the Holy Spirit* (Zondervan)

A. W. Tozer, *The Pursuit of God* (Christian Publications) and *The Knowledge of the Holy* (Christian Publications). Everything Tozer wrote is well worth reading. This man knew God intimately!

Dallas Willard, *The Spirit of the Disciplines* (HarperSanFrancisco)

You'll notice that these authors cover a broad range of centuries and denominations. Regarding the latter, I never dreamed two years ago that I would be having my spiritual socks blessed off by dead Catholics! But I am. As someone raised in an anti-Catholic home and church environment, it's been a joyous surprise to discover that Francois Fenelon, Brother Lawrence, Julian of Norwich, Thomas à Kempis, and others loved Jesus passionately and knew that they were right with God only by his grace. And the writings of priest and professor Henri Nouwen, recently deceased, continually challenge me to know God more intimately and love him more deeply.

For an introduction to devotional writers through the centuries, see Richard Foster and James Smith's *Devotional Classics: Selected Readings for Individuals and Groups* (HarperCollins).

I recently subscribed to the quarterly newsletter published by

Renovare, an organization founded by Richard Foster. Renovare provides resources and information intended to promote spiritual renewal in Christians and the church. For information, contact: Renovare, Inc., 8 Inverness Drive East, Suite 102, Englewood, CO 80112-5609.

When I first began to seek more intimacy with God and greater awareness of his presence, I found it hard to battle distractions and wandering thoughts. Sometimes I still do. Maybe you are finding that a problem, too.

To help me concentrate on Christ's presence, I place an empty chair in front of me and put a favorite drawing of Jesus in it. Currently I'm using the one shown at the end of this appendix. I usually begin by kneeling beside the chair and giving Jesus, my Savior king, praise and adoration. This keeps me conscious of Jesus as Lord even as I concentrate on Jesus as right there with me.

Then I sit comfortably, closing my eyes and breathing deeply to help me relax. As I inhale and exhale slowly, I silently repeat a personalized portion of Scripture, such as "Jesus is with me always. Jesus is here with me now" (see Matthew 28:20) or a biblically based phrase like "Abba, I belong to you." This helps me concentrate on Jesus' presence. And it refocuses my mind on him when (notice I didn't say *if*) distracting thoughts hijack my attention. I also keep a notepad nearby to record concerns I must attend to later. This helps me let go of them and give God my undivided attention.

At the start of my attempts to practice God's presence, I came before him with nothing but my Bible and my prayer journal. I still do that on my one-day retreats. Yet as a person who likes order, I soon realized I wanted a devotional guide of some kind. However, I needed one that had a flexible structure with space to focus on building intimacy with God. As I said in chapter 2, Bob and Michael Benson's *Disciplines for the Inner Life* (Waco, Tex.: Word, 1985) fills that need. The authors suggest letting God's Spirit guide the pace as readers go through the book's fifty topics.

I often repeat a particular theme for several weeks. Each topic includes daily Scripture reading, suggested meditation, and short theme-related passages selected from a broad spectrum of religious authors.

Following this format, I find that most days I read shorter Bible passages than I used to. And I *meditate* more on Scripture now by focusing on one verse or phrase, even if it means I don't get very far in a chapter. I ask God to speak to me *personally* from the verse(s). Often I put myself into the biblical scene, especially when I read from the Gospels. You could say that I'm reading less and enjoying it much more. (As I said in chapter 2, I do in-depth Bible study at a separate time.)

I also spend less time in "asking" prayer than I did before. So from the outside observer's perspective, my morning times likely appear less productive, especially considering that I don't "hear" from God every time I meet with him.

As I focus on God's presence, I'm learning that it's all right to "waste time" with God. I mean that I must set aside my Puritan work ethic, so to speak, when I come to my special place to meet Jesus. This has not been easy for me, but I keep focusing on my primary goal of increasing nearness to God. Besides, time spent focusing on God has value in itself, just because God is God. *We must come to value the wonder of being with God, as his beloved, without doing or hearing anything!*

I share these thoughts with you only as a window into my private time with God. None of the things I do has any power in itself. This is merely the way I have found that I can best worship and be with Christ. And I purposefully am not describing in detail my times with Abba for two reasons. First, they are not always the same in length, format, etc. (And no, I do not have them *every single day* of my life, I regret to say.) But more important, we need to develop our own methods of being alone with Christ Jesus our Lord and drawing closer to him. For you it may be spending time outdoors in a secluded place. You may not feel comfortable kneeling *at all*. Or you may think you ought to kneel *throughout* your time of focusing on God. That's fine. Kneeling isn't important. Building intimacy with God is. The point is for you to find an optimum way to cut out distractions and focus on the presence of your Abba as you speak to him and let him speak to you through his Word and his Spirit. Ask him to lead you into the ways that will work best for you. Trust him to do that. After all, God is the One who planted in your heart the desire to draw nearer to him.

And as you make time to build intimacy with Abba, remember this wise observation by Peter Lord: "My experience with our Lord is that when I begin to associate blessings with behavior [like a certain, set way of having our devotional times] rather than with him, he ceases to bless that behavior. Then I come back and discover that *he, and not my behavior, is the source of all blessings.*" (*Hearing God* [Grand Rapids: Baker, 1988], 201).

Note: The drawing I use is called "I Am Here."

© Thomas R. Golden 1992.

When I show this drawing in the seminars or classes I lead, people often come to me after the session to ask where they can get copies. Anticipating that you might have that same question, I am including the name and address of the distributor of this art piece. For more information, contact: Comfort Prints, P.O. Box 27513, Santa Ana, CA 92799-7513, phone 800/964-1116.

Chapter 1: "Why Do I Have a Hole in My Soul?"

1. In this and all subsequent stories, I've altered names and details beyond recognition.

2. See, for example, Marilyn Elias, "Parents' Loving Feeling Isn't Lost on Children," *USA Today*, 19 April, 1991. Elias reports research that followed seventy-six children from early childhood into adult life. It demonstrated how children's emotions, attitudes, and relational patterns were shaped by their parents' relational patterns. Parents' displays of affection and warmth strongly predicted closer marriages and friendships along with better mental health and successful future careers. Researchers offered two likely causes for the link between the quality of the parents' relationships and their children's later social skills. Children may learn the behavior their parents modeled and use it as adults. And children "with affectionate parents may also develop a sense of internal security that enables them to socially engage other people."

Also see J. J. Lynch, *The Broken Heart: The Medical Consequences of Loneliness* (New York: Basic Books, 1977). This book reports research demonstrating that, in comparison to men who had caring relationships, men who were lonely died at a younger age, even when all other risk factors were considered.

3. Frederick Buechner, *The Longing for Home* (San Francisco: HarperSanFrancisco, 1996), 18–19.

4. Paul Smith, as quoted in Gary Moon, *Homesick for Eden* (Franklin Springs, Ga.: LifeSprings Resources, 1966), 43.

Chapter 2: "Why Do I Try So Hard but Change So Little?"

1. Sandra D. Wilson, *Released from Shame* (Downers Grove, Ill.: InterVarsity Press, 1990), 123.

2. My thanks to Pat Springle for the ideas in this paragraph.

3. Human counselors can play a very important part—but only a part. Let's face it, we usually have a counselor present with us only a few hours a month at best. Ideally, we have or can find other people to speak truth to us too. A thriving church may be the best place to find those people, especially a church with support groups or some type of discipling or mentoring program.

4. Gary Moon, *Homesick for Eden* (Ann Arbor, Mich.: Servant, 1997).

5. The apostle Paul often uses the imagery of athletic training or discipline as part of the believer's life. For example, 1 Timothy 4:7 instructs us, "Spend your time and energy in training yourself for spiritual fitness." And Peter writes to Christians about "supplying" or "applying" specific spiritual habits (e.g., "moral excellence," "self-control," "love for other Christians") to the faith that had already saved them and made them able to "share in his divine nature." And Peter exhorts believers to "practice these things" (see 2 Peter 1:3-10, NASB).

   In *The Spirit of the Disciplines,* Southern Baptist pastor and seminary professor Dallas Willard divides the classic spiritual habits into Disciplines of Abstinence (e.g., solitude, silence, fasting) and Disciplines of Engagement (e.g., study, worship, service, prayer, fellowship). Other writers, both ancient and contemporary, compose different lists. But all seek to draw from the practices and words of Christ and the New Testament writers.

6. Robert McGee and Rujon Morrison, *From Head to Heart* (Ann Arbor, Mich.: Vine Books, 1997). This idea of settling for a defini-

tion *about* God in place of a relationship *with* God permeates McGee and Morrison's fine book.

7. I use phrases like "practicing the presence of God" and "cultivating intimacy with Christ" interchangeably. Theologians through the ages have failed to plumb the depths of mystery inherent in the triune Godhead: Father, Son, and Holy Spirit. So I won't even try! In my special times with God, I usually focus on the actual presence of Jesus, who is with me (as well as in me, by the Holy Spirit) and simultaneously "sits at God's right hand" (Col. 3:1). Sometimes I talk to my heavenly Father, Jesus, and the Holy Spirit in the same prayer. I apologize if this is confusing. (I'm convinced that God has no trouble keeping it straight.)

8. Quoted in Eddie Ensley, *Prayer That Heals Our Emotions* (San Francisco: Harper & Row, 1988), 10.

9. Ibid.

10. Andrew Murray, *With Christ in the School of Prayer* (Old Tappan, N. J.: Fleming H. Revell, 1972), 124.

11. The phrase "descend with my mind into my heart" is used by Anthony M. Coniaris in his book *Discovering God through the Daily Practice of His Presence* (Minneapolis: Light and Life Publishing, 1989), 9.

12. C. S. Lewis, "First and Second Things," in *Readings for Meditation and Reflection,* edited by Walter Hooper (San Francisco: HarperCollins, 1992), 14.

13. From *Knowing God* by J. I. Packer, as quoted in Bob and Michael Benson's *Disciplines for the Inner Life* (Nashville: Word, 1985), 77 (emphasis added).

14. Joseph S. Carroll, *How to Worship Jesus Christ* (Chicago: Moody Press, 1984), 19.

Chapter 3: "How Can I Get Close to a God I Don't Trust?"

1. A. W. Tozer, *The Knowledge of the Holy* (San Francisco: HarperSanFrancisco, 1992), 1.

2. I wrote about this in *Shame-Free Parenting* (Downers Grove, Ill.: InterVarsity Press, 1992).

3. H. Norman Wright, "Always Daddy's Girl," *Focus on the Family* (February 1990): 2–5.

4. From Dietrich Bonhoeffer's *Life Together,* as quoted in Bob and Michael Benson's *Disciplines for the Inner Life* (Waco, Tex.: Word, 1985), 59–60.

5. Frederick Buechner, *The Magnificent Defeat* (San Francisco: Harper & Row, 1966), 135.

6. Kenneth Leech, *True Prayer,* as quoted in Bob and Michael Benson's *Disciplines for the Inner Life* (Waco, Tex.: Word, 1985), 20 (emphasis added).

7. A. W. Tozer, *The Knowledge of the Holy* (San Francisco: HarperSanFrancisco, 1992), 14–15 (emphasis added). Tozer credits the last two lines to poet Frederick W. Faber.

8. Ibid., 67.

Chapter 4: "How Can I Find and Accept the Real Me?"

1. Peter Lord, *Soul Care* (Grand Rapids: Baker, 1990), 37.

2. Harold Kushner, "You Don't Have to Be Perfect to Be Loved," *Parade Magazine* (8 September 1996): 18–9.

3. Brennan Manning, *The Ragamuffin Gospel* (Sisters, Ore.: Multnomah, 1990), 182.

4. Brennan Manning, *Abba's Child* (Colorado Springs, Colo.: NavPress, 1994), 51.

5. Manning, *The Ragamuffin Gospel,* 21, 188.

6. Ibid., 136.

7. Henri Nouwen, as quoted in Manning, *Abba's Child,* 50.

Chapter 5: "How Do I Risk Letting Others See the Real Me?"

1. Ruthellen Josselson, *The Space between Us* (San Francisco: Jossey-Bass, 1992), 47.

2. While this quiz has no verified validity, it has served to suggest our tendencies to protect ourselves by using a certain mask style.

3. John Courtright and Sid Rogers, "Surviving Your Spouse's Recovery Journey," *Steps* (Winter 1994/95): 5, 8.

4. Dale Ryan and Juanita Ryan, *Rooted in God's Love* (Downers Grove, Ill.: InterVarsity, 1992), 17–8.

5. Deuteronomy 33:27 (NIV).

Chapter 6: "How Can I Be Secure Enough to Reach Out to Others?"

1. For a more extensive discussion of how we hurt one another relationally and what to do about it, see Sandra D. Wilson, *Hurt People Hurt People* (Nashville: Thomas Nelson, 1993).

2. Sandra D. Wilson, *Shame-Free Parenting* (Downers Grove, Ill.: InterVarsity, 1992).

Chapter 7: "How Do I Get Past the Pain, Forgive, and Move On?"

1. Kim Sue Lia Perkes, "A Place to Park Pain," *The Arizona Republic,* 6 March 1996.

2. Gordon Dalbey, "The Cry for Daddy," *Focus on the Family* (September 1996): 3–4.

3. Deidre Donahue, "Bly Shakes His Finger at a Nation That Refuses to Grow Up," *USA Today,* 28 June 1996.

4. Philip Yancey, "Does It Matter? Does God Care?" *Christianity Today* (22 November 1993): 20–23.

5. Jeff VanVonderen, *Tired of Trying to Measure Up* (Minneapolis: Bethany House, 1989), 151.

6. I wrote this poem several years ago. It first appeared in *Hurt People Hurt People* (Nashville: Thomas Nelson, 1993), 198.

7. Beverly described this high school graduation experience as a "fantasy" because her father had died six years earlier. She was not asking the Holy Spirit to change her past. God does not alter the facts of our pasts. But he has the power to change our perceptions and feelings about those facts. Beverly told me that she believes God let her experience her father's pride over *what she accomplished* (her academic success) in this way so that she could contrast it with her Abba's love for *who she is* (his beloved child) unrelated to her grade average. Beverly realized that although she always wanted her daddy to be proud of her report card, she longed far more for him to love her just because she was his little girl.

8. Quoted in Richard Lee, *Windows to the Heart of God* (Eugene, Ore.: Harvest House, 1996), 204.

9. NIV.

Chapter 8: "I'm Home Where I Belong."

1. "Adopted Boys Accused of Stealing, Blowing $10,000," *The Arizona Republic,* 23 June 1995.

2. Brennan Manning, *The Ragamuffin Gospel* (Sisters, Ore.: Multnomah, 1990), 197.

3. Siang-Yang Tan and Douglas Gregg, *Disciplines of the Holy Spirit* (Grand Rapids: Zondervan, 1997), 224.

4. Walter J. Burghardt, *Tell the Next Generation* (New York: Paulist Press, 1980), 43.

5. E. Stanley Jones as quoted in Tricia McCary Rhodes, *The Soul at Rest* (Minneapolis: Bethany House, 1996), 88.

Sandra D. Wilson, Ph.D., is a family therapist, internationally sought speaker, and author of six books, including *Released from Shame.* Sandy is a Phi Beta Kappa scholar and summa cum laude graduate of the University of Cincinnati with a master's degree from the University of Louisville and a doctorate in counseling psychology from the Union Institute. She holds visiting professor status at Associated Canadian Theological Schools, Denver Conservative Baptist Seminary, and Trinity Evangelical Divinity School. Sandy also serves on the advisory boards of the National Association for Christian Recovery and Equipping Ministries International and on the executive board of the American Association of Christian Counselors.

Sandy Wilson's love for God and his Word permeates all of her work. Her writing flows from more than her experience as a Christian therapist and teacher. As an adult child of an alcoholic and as a survivor of childhood sexual abuse, Sandy shares openly from her personal healing experience.

Sandy and her husband, Garth, have been married for forty years and are the proud parents of two grown children and the doting grandparents of four "astoundingly bright and beautiful" grandchildren. Sandy and Garth live in Scottsdale, Arizona.

To schedule Sandy Wilson for retreats and conferences that focus on cultivating intimacy with Christ, contact her at (602) 502-0723.

Other AACC-Tyndale books include

Family Shock: Keeping Families Strong in the Midst of Earthshaking Change by Gary R. Collins, Ph.D.

Intimate Allies: Rediscovering God's Design for Marriage and Becoming Soul Mates for Life by Dan B. Allender, Ph.D., and Tremper Longman III, Ph.D.

"Why Did You Do That?" Understand Why Your Family Members Act as They Do by Wm. Lee Carter, Ed.D.

Questions Couples Ask behind Closed Doors: A Christian Counselor Explores the Most Common Conflicts of Marriage by James Osterhaus, Ph.D.

High-Maintenance Relationships: How to Handle Impossible People by Les Parrott III, Ph.D.

Fresh Start: 8 Principles for Starting Over When a Relationship Doesn't Work by Thomas Whiteman, Ph.D., and Randy Petersen

Simplify Your Life and Get More out of It by H. Norman Wright, M.A.

SOON TO BE RELEASED

Breathless: Transforming Your Time-Starved Days into a Life Well Lived by Gary R. Collins, Ph.D.

Changing Your Child's Heart by Steve Sherbondy

On the Threshold of Hope: Opening the Door to Healing for Survivors of Sexual Abuse by Diane Mandt Langberg, Ph.D.

Books in the AACC Counseling Library

Psychology, Theology, and Spirituality in Christian Counseling by Mark R. McMinn, Ph.D.

Counseling Children through the World of Play by Daniel S. Sweeney, Ph.D.

Promoting Change through Brief Therapy in Christian Counseling by Gary J. Oliver, Ph.D., Monte Hasz, Psy.D., and Matthew Richburg, M.A.

Counseling Survivors of Sexual Abuse by Diane Mandt Langberg, Ph.D.